BEYOND THE PIR PANJAL

BEYOND THE PIR PANJAL

LIFE AND MISSIONARY ENTERPRISE IN KASHMIR

ERNEST F. NEVE, M.D., F.R.C.S. (EDIN.)

GYAN

Published by

GYAN

Gyan Publishing House
5, Ansari Road
Daryaganj, New Delhi-110002
Phone: 011-47034999, 9811692060
E-mail: books@gyanbooks.com

Distribution Network
gyanbooks.com
India, USA, Canada, UK, Australia, France

ISBN: 978-81-212-8905-4 (PB)
First Published, 1912

2nd Impression 2023

Printed at: Gyan Press, Delhi.

BEYOND THE PIR PANJAL

AUTHOR: ERNEST F. NEVE

Photo by] [*R. D. Chadda.*

1. CROSSING THE INDUS ON A RAFT OF INFLATED SHEEPSKINS.

BEYOND THE PIR PANJAL

LIFE AND MISSIONARY ENTERPRISE IN KASHMIR

BY

ERNEST F. NEVE, M.D., F.R.C.S. (EDIN.)

CHURCH MISSIONARY SOCIETY

SALISBURY SQUARE, LONDON, E.C.

1915

First Edition 1912
Popular Edition 1914
" " *2nd Impression* . . 1915

PREFACE

THE writer has enjoyed the privilege of living and working in Kashmir for more than a quarter of a century.

During this period, the country has undergone great changes. The most rapid progress was doubtless made in the decade preceeding the year 1900. Politically, Kashmir is very backward, but a great work of preparation is going on. In spite of religious intolerance and social and official opposition, the Spirit of Christ is moving in the land, and the future holds in store spiritual blessings to which hitherto Kashmir, with its unhappy history of tyranny and religious persecution, has been a stranger.

In the chapters on the Mission Hospital, the School and District Work, I have endeavoured to show that the efforts of the Church Missionary Society have been fruitful, although the sphere is one of great difficulty. Much important educational work has been done. The moral and physical condition of the people has been greatly improved. In this work, the Mission has had a large share. The medical branch, in addition to its wide-spread ministry of healing, has been especially effective in delivering the great message of Christianity.

I have tried also to show the happy and useful life's work and the great opportunities for service which are possible to Christian medical men in the East.

If what I have written should inspire any qualified men or women, doctors or nurses, to take up such work as their career, the time spent in writing these pages will have been indeed worth while.

In the description of the manifold activities of the Mission School, I have in places quoted freely from the racy annual reports of that great Scout-master, the Rev. Cecil Tyndale-Biscoe.

Most of the illustrations are from my own photographs. Those which are not I have acknowledged, and am grateful for permission to use them.

I will only add that I am fully aware of the literary and other shortcomings of the following pages.

CONTENTS

CONTENTS

LIST OF ILLUSTRATIONS

BEYOND THE PIR PANJAL

CHAPTER I

THE VALE OF KASHMIR

Spring Beauties—The Pir Panjal Range—Konsa Nág—Gulmarg—The Ascent of Mount Tatticooti—The Basin of the Jhelum River—Its Source — Vernag — Achibal — Báwan — Picturesque Islamabad — A Medical Mission—Ancient Temple of Martand.

> A vale of purple glens and snow-cold streams,
> Broad meadows lush with verdure, flower and fruit,
> The broad-leafed maple towering in his pride,
> The temple's noble ruin on the height;
> The poplar lines that mark the homestead there,
> Calm lakes that bear the lotus on their breast.
>
> C. R. TOLLEMACHE.

KASHMIR owes much of its fame to its varied phases of beauty. These are partly due to the seasons. But the different altitudes, with their countless slopes and upland meadows, some with northern and others with southern aspect, continually provide a simultaneous presentation of the beauties of successive seasons. In the hottest summer weather, for instance, when in the valley the temperature is over 90° F. in the shade, when the air is laden with moisture and mosquitoes abound, a ride or drive of 30 miles and a climb of 3000 feet will take us to where the atmosphere is fresh and cool. Another two or three thousand feet of ascent will bring us to snow and to early spring flowers such as primulas and anemones. And looking down from the heights to the plain below, with its masses of foliage dimly discernible in the midst of the heat haze, we appreciate the effect of altitude on climate.

In the valley, in early spring, sheets of white and pale pink almond blossom on the hillsides dip down into broad stretches of brilliant yellow mustard. The landscape is full of colour. The tender green of young wheat contrasts with the rich madder brown of newly-ploughed fields. Innumerable willows with orange-coloured branches and pale yellow-green feathery foliage are massed together in the hollows or form lines across the landscape. In the distance is the deep blue of the foot-hills, with above them the pure white surface and serrated crest of lofty mountains still mantled in winter snow, upon which there is perpetual play of sunshine chasing shadow.

The almond blossom has hardly passed its climax of beauty and sprinkled the turf below with its petals before the snowy white of the flowering apricot trees in gardens and orchards becomes conspicuous; and then the peach trees put forth their exquisite pink blossom, which, with the sun shining through, stands out brilliantly against the azure sky. Flocks of birds, which during the winter had sought warmer climes, now return to Kashmir. Others, which have silently borne the winter snow and frost, find their voices and at dawn the song of thrushes and blackbirds mingles with the rich tones of the golden oriole and the air vibrates with the melody of the countless feathered inhabitants of every large tree.

Springing grass has now clothed the earth-covered roofs of the houses, on some of which till recently there were masses of orange-red crown imperial lilies, while here and there flashes the gorgeous scarlet of clusters of large Moghul tulips. In the midst of the soft velvety turf are clumps of white and purple iris, the scent of which mingles with that of the May bushes, which are in full blossom. The beauty of this season appeals to every sense.

The Vale of Kashmir may be described as an oval basin 80 miles long and 20 broad, extending from south-east to north-west. It is girt by mighty mountain ranges, many of the peaks of which are higher than Mont Blanc. These are the pearls which encircle the emerald valley.

Although the mountain wall appears continuous and unbroken, the contour of the oval is irregular and interrupted by projecting ridges and receding valleys. The most important of these usher down the tributaries of the Jhelum, of which on the right bank the chief are the Lidar, Sind and Pohru rivers, and on the left or south-west bank the Veshau and Dudhganga. At the point where these debouch into the valley there are extensive fan-shaped expanses, miles across and terraced with rice-fields.

The Jhelum pursues a winding course, not down the centre of the valley, but near the north-east side. The right bank, owing to its sloping southern aspect, is drier and warmer, and the crops ripen earlier than those of the left bank and south side. One striking physical peculiarity of Kashmir is the fact that the southern slopes of the ranges, where the snow melts quickly, are treeless and bare. They are covered with long grass, which, as the summer advances, becomes very dry. Accidental fires sometimes cause great destruction and sweep over large areas, still further accentuating and perpetuating the bareness. Slopes with a northern aspect, where the snow lingers longer, are on the other hand green and forest-clad, and the afforestation naturally promotes still further the retention of moisture and frequency of rainfall. This is also the case in those of the outlying valleys which run east and west.

On either side of the Jhelum throughout its length there is an extended area of flat alluvial plain, from one to five miles in width. And from the foot of the great boundary ranges, the high ground gradually shelves down to join this plain. So that although the river banks and the plain around are only a little over 5000 feet above sea-level, a very large part of the valley of Kashmir has an altitude of over 6000 feet. The Pir Panjal range is a serrated edge of rocky arête-joined peaks and snow-clad slopes. It forms the highest line of the great mountain barrier which divides Kashmir from the plains of Northern India.

Approaching it from the valley of Kashmir, which lies to the east, we gradually rise, passing first through broken plateaus, fissured and eroded by water. Up these intersecting valleys the path passes, until at a height of about 6000 feet we begin to see occasional pines. A gradual ascent for a few more hundred feet brings us to the lower margin of the great fir forest which clothes the foot of the Pir Panjal slopes with a band about 80 miles long, and with an average breadth of perhaps 6 miles. In spite of the extent to which this forest is overrun by herdsmen, it still remains the haunt of black bear. Large streams flowing down from the snows pierce it in many places, and the easiest routes to those snows are usually to be found along the sides of these torrent valleys.

Some of the summits are of great beauty, such as the three Brahma peaks at the south-east end of the range, whose graceful conical forms, the lower shoulders of which are mantled with perpetual snow, tower up to a height of 15,500 feet. Four thousand feet lower down, nestling at their base, lies the turquoise-blue Konsa Nág, a glacier-fed lake 3 miles in length (Plate 2). This is the source of the Veshau River. The ascent to Konsa Nág is made from near Shupeyon, up a long valley past the fine Haribal Falls. The final climb is for 1000 feet up a grass-covered moraine. The lake then comes into view, lying in a hollow on the south side of the main peaks.

Along the slopes of the great mountain range which bounds Kashmir to the south there is a continuous series of "margs," between seven and nine thousand feet above sea-level. These are stretches of upland flowery meadow occupying the depressions between the fir-covered slopes and ridges of the higher foot-hills and the crest of the main range. The exact mode of formation of these margs is not quite evident. No doubt originally they were glacier-filled,

Photo by] [*Shiv Nath.*

2. KONSA NÁG.

(A glacier-fed lake at the foot of the Brahma Peaks.)

and even now the winter snow lingers on in their trough-like hollows. But they have rich soil, and it is not clear as to why they have not become covered by the forest which borders them, and which in many places has sent out little groups and lines of firs and pines which stand out boldly in the midst of the pasturage around. At present the extensive grazing of herds and flocks, especially of goats, is fatal to the growth of young trees.

Gulmarg, the favourite summer resort of Europeans, with its church, hotel and bazaar, its club, polo-ground, golf links and its numerous wooden huts, is one of many of these green valleys with undulating slopes. Situated 3000 feet above the valley level, its climate is delightful. To this and its accessibility it owes its selection and popularity, for it is only 30 miles by road from Srinagar. Some of the houses are built on the long fir-clothed ridge which overlooks the plain. From Gulmarg there is a magnificent view of the valley of Kashmir and the mountains to the north, Mahadeo, Kotwal, Haramouk, and in the distance an outstanding snowy range culminating in the beautiful peak of Nanga Parbat, the eighth highest mountain in the world.

Evening after evening these mountains and the nearer peaks of the Ferozepore valley are bathed in glorious sunset colours.

There is a succession of margs all along the Pir Panjal range. And one of the most beautiful expeditions in Kashmir is to march along at the marg level, camping day after day in exquisitely beautiful spots. All around are stretches of grassy meadow spangled with flowers, among which columbines, balsams, anemones, larkspurs and dwarf sunflowers are conspicuous.

Above and below is the great forest, through which there are frequent glimpses of the long glittering white line above and the far-flung valley below.

During May and early June, before it becomes unpleasantly warm, Srinagar is full of European visitors, who have flocked in to Kashmir to escape the heat of the Plains of India. After the middle of June a great exodus occurs to Gulmarg, the season of which lasts till about the middle of September. During these three months Gulmarg is a gay Anglo-Indian hill station.

After the second week of September, with the return of the British Resident from Gulmarg, Srinagar again becomes the centre of European interest. During the bright dry autumn weather, however, many visitors make camping expeditions or travel about in house-boats.

To the west of the Brahma peaks the Sedau and Pir Panjal passes cross the range in two well-marked gaps, separated by a group of five grey rocky summits which enclose snowfields of considerable extent. Looking along the sky-line, again 6 miles to the west, is the highest point of the whole range—Sunset Peak, so named because it is the last of the tops to catch the rays of the setting sun. This peak has a saddle-back, and has been several times ascended by Dr Arthur Neve, myself and various friends. The ascent, which is not difficult, lies for the last three hours up a snow slope, which gradually increases in steepness and culminates in a rocky arête, the southern face of which, and of the peak itself, drops as a sheer precipice for some hundreds of feet. On the summit pieces of smooth rock with vitreous fracture can be found, showing bubbles and other traces of igneous action.

The most conspicuous and imposing of all the peaks of the Pir Panjal range is undoubtedly Tatticooti (Plate 3), the pyramidal shape of which, with a central notch and very steep and jagged western and northern sides, makes it look as if it might be exceedingly difficult to ascend. In 1900 I made an attempt, and succeeded in attaining a point about three-quarters of the way up the final peak, and well above the apex of the notch. The obstacles were, however, too many. My camp was far away, and the fatigue great. The peak became shrouded by cloud, and the porters refused to

3. VIEW OF MOUNT TATTICOOTH FROM THE SOUTH.
(The height of the portion shown is about 2,500 feet.)

proceed. However, I found, as I believed, a good and practicable route. On 6th August 1901 the late Rev. C. E. Barton and I pitched our tents above the pines of the Sangsofed River. On 7th August we did 5 miles of steady ascent, at first through birches and juniper bushes, and then over grassy and flowery meadows, bright with crown gentians and golden potentillas and dotted with great boulders. Climbing a grass-covered terminal moraine, 250 feet in height, we placed our base camp on a stretch of meadow under a rounded knoll, the rocky faces of which were ground and polished by the ice of ages. Our altitude was then 10,850 feet.

The following day 2 miles ascent, chiefly climbing and scrambling over moraine, brought us on to the snowfield, part of the continuous névé, from which the Pir Panjal peaks in a long line lift their rocky heads. Here our direction changed from south to west, and emerging from the head of the valley we finally took a north-westerly course along the surface of the snowfield, steadily rising until we reached the upper level, near the southern arête of Tatticooti, the height attained being 12,850 feet. Here we pitched two shelter tents on the rocks, one for ourselves, the other for the porters. The weather was very unsettled and at intervals there was hail and a driving wind, the peaks being almost entirely in cloud, but occasionally clearing for a few minutes. About 10 p.m. a violent storm set in with drifting snow, and for some time after midnight and in the early morning our tents were in danger from the violence of the blast. And we passed a very disturbed night holding on to the tent poles. On the morning of the 9th it cleared by 8 o'clock and the sun came out, and shone brilliantly upon three inches of fresh snow. Our tent ropes were coated with ice and the canvas covered by a layer of frozen snow. The peak was quite clear, and in spite of the late hour the outlook was decidedly promising. Crossing the south-eastern arête, we were compelled to descend 300 feet to a snowfield covering the eastern glacier. The steep slope, with loose rocks and fresh snow, resting in places on ice, caused some delay here, but by 10.30 we had crossed the snowfield and reached the foot of a broad couloir stretching 600 feet up to the north-eastern arête. We started off on snow, but above we had to scramble up a very steep shale slope. At the top was a cornice of snow with the 5 feet edge towards us. On the opposite (northern) side a very sharp snow incline extended straight away down for two or three thousand feet to a glacier.

From the point where we stood, a broken and steep rocky arête stretched up for more than 2000 feet towards the summit, which could not be seen. Following up the arête for a short distance, we worked across its northern face amongst loose rocks and fresh snow, traversing some couloirs full of snow, continuous with the steep slope below. We rejoined the main arête about 200 feet higher, and a steady steep climb up the edge brought us at last to a point at which it became knife-like. By working down a ledge on its southern side we reached a couloir which, steadily followed up, eventually brought us again to the main arête, only a few hundred feet below the top. The gradient then became less severe, although the drop on both sides was very great. The porters caused some trouble and delay, owing to their being unused to the rope.

We reached the summit (15,524 feet) at 2 p.m. It was very sharp, being formed by two blocks of trap rock standing on end, immediately below which was a vein of pure white quartz. We believe this to be the first time that the summit of Tatticooti has been reached.

The Pir Panjal has its seasons. In midwinter it is covered by deep pure snow of dazzling whiteness, with which the black cliffs and vertical faces of rock, the serrated edges and the splintered crests of the ridges show up in sharp contrast. Long gently curved lines of snowfield stand out clearly against the sky. Deep cobalt-coloured shadows lie on the mountain side, and are prolonged downwards into an atmosphere of mauve, which drapes the lower slopes. All the upland meadows, the margs and high valleys, are completely enveloped by a white mantle many feet deep, and the band of dark forest is speckled with the snow which rests on and weighs down the branches of countless firs and pines.

In the spring, melting takes place very rapidly. By the end of February the valley of Kashmir is always free of snow, and day by day the line recedes up the foot of the hills. A few days of warm sunshine clears the trees. The southern slopes of the margs soon become bare and stretches of upland pasturage often present a rippled appearance. This is due to the melting of the snow on the south side of all inequalities in the ground, while that on the north side remains. A bank, a tuft of grass, a furrow or clod—all act as cover to the snow and help to prolong its stay. But soon all is gone and the upper slopes begin to show, first as light brown and then as green patches. And when the spring sun is shining, great sheets of the melting snowfields above, like mirrors, reflect the dazzling light. Backwards and upwards retreats the snow line, exposing first the fringe, and then the masses of piled-up moraine which fills the upper end of each tributary valley.

In the autumn the old snow is almost entirely melted on the Pir Panjal range, leaving a series of grey rounded glaciers, streaked with watercourses and resting in the hollows between the peaks and main ridges.

The spring flowers are all gone. In their places we see tufted spikes of the rich red *polygonum*, the tall lavender-like *stachys*, the dwarf mauve *swertia*, and a *delphinium* with large cowl-shaped flowers. Everlastings and edelweiss are still abundant. Above the forest the slopes are clothed with miles of juniper bush in dense dark green patches among which red, orange and yellow clumps of euphorbia with oleander-like leaves form beautiful masses of colour.

On the higher peaks the last flower to be seen is the *Great Saussurea*, like a globe of white velvet the size of a cricket ball, the contour studded with violet blossoms, each about half an inch across, which project slightly from the surface. The whole rests in the centre of a rosette of foliage (Plate 4). It is a most curious flower and greatly prized by the people, who call it the king of medicines. Decoctions of it form a bland and soothing drink which the Kashmiris say is agreeable and helpful in catarrhal affections of the digestive and respiratory tracts.

To approach the glacier, whereas in the spring we could walk up slopes of hard snow, we have now to climb over long stretches of moraine.

These ice-fields are wonderful in the autumn. In the early morning before sunrise all the moisture is locked up by frost. So keen is the cold even in the first week of September that the inside of one's tent sparkles with rime and looks like the interior of a salt-mine. Walking on the glaciers at this time is difficult, if the slope is more than 20°, as in many places the ice is perfectly smooth. Where the surface is slightly honeycombed it is easier. Absolute silence reigns. Not a sound is to be heard at this early hour. Having done our climb, on the return journey there is a vast change.

In the early morning the sun rose in a cloudless sky. Now fleecy clouds have gathered and tend to drift across the higher peaks. The sunshine is hot and the silent glacier of the forenoon has become alive with sound and motion. Everywhere is the roaring sound of water. Torrents are pouring down the icy slopes. The whole surface is wet and glittering with the movement of water. Miniature avalanches occur ever and anon on the steeper faces where snow has remained, and falling stones are frequent. All the streams are swollen and laden with débris. These diurnal variations are at their height during the month of September, when the great sun heat of the day is succeeded by frost at night and

4. THE GREAT SAUSSUREA (SAUSSUREA GOSSYPIPHORA).

the range of temperature between day and night often exceeds 100° F.

From the summit of Mount Tatticooti the view is most impressive. Stretched out below us is the whole length of the Vale of Kashmir with the winding, glittering Jhelum. So sinuous is the river that some of its loops, three or four miles long, have necks which are less than quarter of a mile across. From Vernag, its source, to the point where it leaves the valley the Jhelum is 122 miles long, although the distance by road is only 80 miles.

The Banihal route to Jammu is the nearest and the most direct to the Punjab. It leaves the valley at Vernag. A few years ago a railway to India was on the point of being constructed from here. It is greatly to be regretted that the scheme was abandoned and that for political reasons this road has been practically closed to ordinary traffic.

At the point at which it leaves the valley to cross the Banihal Pass and join the Chenáb valley at Rámband, there is a beautiful garden. This was planted by the Emperor Jehangir, whose favourite residence it became and who desired to be carried there when dying. Amid avenues of lofty chenar trees[1] are bubbling springs and crystal streams. And at the upper end, under the shadow of a steep pine-clad limestone scarp, lies a deep quiet octagonal pool of dark blue water, 125 feet across, bounded by blocks of shaped stone and surrounded by an ancient wall of masonry with arched recesses. This tank is crowded with sacred fish, some of which attain a considerable size. When crumbs are thrown to them they come together and form a seething mass of brown backs and gleaming yellow sides as they struggle for the food.

This pool is the source of the Jhelum. From it issues a clear, sparkling stream, which passes under an old balconied building by which it is spanned. It flows down the centre

[1] Platanus Orientalis. These magnificent plane trees attain a size much greater than that of the largest English elms.

of the garden, below which it falls as a cascade and is augmented by other springs among which is the Veth Vatru, which although much smaller is regarded by the Hindus as the true source of the Veth, as they call the Jhelum.

About 9 miles from Vernag, somewhat to the right of the direct route to Islamabad, a ridge juts into the valley from the northern range and terminates in the pointed cedar-covered Sosanwar Hill. On the northern slope of this is Achibal, another of Jehangir's beautiful gardens, with lines of chenars, between which flows a clear stream, trained into a broad stone-lined channel with square tanks and fountains fed by the copious springs which gush out of the hillside above.

At many places round the valley there are similar large springs, most of them enclosed by tanks which contain sacred fish. There is usually limestone in the immediate vicinity. And very often in the neighbouring villages goître is common. Such tanks have probably been regarded with reverence from olden days. Many are overshadowed by ancient elm trees at the foot of which stand one or more Hindu images daubed with red paint. In the "Ain Akbari" it is stated that in 700 places in Kashmir there were carved figures of snakes, worshipped by Hindus, and most of these were associated with springs. After Vernag rank the sacred ponds at Báwan, near Martand. There is also a beautiful old Hindu sacred pool at Tregám at the west end of the valley.

One of the most ancient forms of worship in Kashmir was that of the pixies, who were believed to live in the water. These are called Nágs. And they were supposed to assume the form of a snake, which enabled them to creep through the hidden mountain channels and emerge at the springs. Sometimes, like mermaids, they are said to have assumed human form and to have been recognized by the water which dripped from their locks. Curious legends are told of them. "There is a well-known spring, Vaishak Nág, the water of which is light and sweet. In the early part of May the wind blows violently for three days and the water appears. In October the water dries up and departs to the Jammu side of the mountains for the winter. This happened in the following way. A holy man from the Jammu side, who deplored the absence of water, came to Vaishak Nág and by good fortune caught the snake, the lord of the spring, and put it in his gourd; while returning thanks he hung his gourd on a tree. Two women coming by thought the gourd might contain butter for anointing their hair, and took the gourd down, whereupon the snake escaped. The holy man returned and discovered his loss. As he stood weeping, Mir Shah Baghdadi appeared, who, moved by the holy man's distress, effected a compromise with the snake. So it comes to pass that Kashmir gets its water for its rice crop, while the Jammu villages receive water for their spring crops."[1]

The Kashmiri name for a spring is Nág, which is also the word for snake. The cult of springs still goes on. One of the favourite Hindu goddesses is Kir Bhawani. And Tula Mula, the great spring of this goddess, is regarded by many as the most sacred place in Kashmir. It is situated at the mouth of the Sind valley. The water is of a dark blue colour. The Hindus say that when famine or cholera is impending, the water changes its tint and becomes darker.

From Islamabad the river becomes navigable for 100 miles, to a short distance below Baramula. On this great waterway Islamabad is the eastern and Baramula the western terminus. Between these and on its banks are most of the larger towns and many villages. Srinagar itself lies about the centre.

Islamabad, called by the Hindus Anant Nág, is the second largest town in Kashmir, and has a population of about 10,500. It is clustered round the foot of a conical hill—a

[1] Lawrence, *Valley of Kashmir.*

huddle of earthen grass-covered roofs resting on wooden frameworks, filled in with sun-dried bricks and plastered with smooth grey or pale yellow mud. The general effect of the town is most picturesque. It is embowered in apple and pear orchards and traversed by numerous springs. Some of these pour out from the foot of the hill and flow into gardens under lofty chenar trees and past temples where there are tanks full of sacred fish. Others, some of them sulphurous, bubble up by the roadside in square stone-lined pools, with steps leading down to the water's edge. And rippling streams flow along the sides of the streets. Many of the houses are old-fashioned, with quaint latticed verandahs and balconies (Plate 5). The roads are paved with rough slabs of stone. Here and there is a line of bakers' shops, with large thin flat chupattis and all sorts of wheaten cakes for sale. A little further on we pass through the blacksmiths' quarter and hear the clang of the hammer as red-hot iron bars are being shaped into ploughshares or axeheads.

At Sop and Kothair, a few miles away, there are quantities of iron ore on the hillside. This used to be smelted in primitive charcoal furnaces, worked with hand bellows. But the industry is no longer carried on. The amount of ore is fairly abundant. It seems a pity that the mines should not be worked under proper management. Although there is no coal, there should be no difficulty in obtaining an ample supply of charcoal for small smelting furnaces.

About twelve miles above Báwan is the village of Eishmakám, with a picturesque Mohammedan shrine on the hillside. It is said that from this mountain King Zain-ul-abul-Din succeeded in obtaining sufficient copper to defray his private expenditure.

In olden days one-fifth of the shawl-weaving of Kashmir was done in Islamabad. The weaving and braiding of floor and table cloths, which is still carried on, is the sole remains of a once flourishing industry.

There is a branch here of the Srinagar Mission School,

Photo by] [R. E. Shorter.

5. A STREET IN ISLÁMABÁD.

and Miss Coverdale is doing quiet educational work among the girls. Immediately outside the road to Báwan is the C.M.S. Mission Hospital for Women, a pretty building of grey stone and red brick, on an excellent site most kindly given by H.H. the Maharajah for the purpose.

This is worked by Miss M. Gomery, M.D., of the Church Missionary Society, with the help of a trained lady nurse, Miss K. Newnham. In 1909 nearly 16,000 visits were paid by patients, and in 1910 Dr Gomery did valuable work in the terrible cholera epidemic.

This institution is becoming increasingly popular and has been bringing a steady influence for good to bear upon the whole town.

Three miles east of Islamabad, on the great plateau which joins the Islamabad Hill to the mountain range which bounds the left bank of the Lidar River, are the ruins of Martand, the most famous of Kashmir temples.

The site is absolutely unique. Behind us are the limestone ridges, which run round to the north to form the cliffs of Báwan. But in front and right and left is a prospect which can be nowhere matched. We look down on to vast expanses of light green and gold and dark green and brown plains and valleys streaked with gleams and flashes of light playing on the flooded rice-fields, the winding river and its tributaries. Further away are mauve-coloured slopes, blue ridges and stretches of faint grey haze, obscuring the distance, and beyond all a complete circle of snows with a few banks of fleecy clouds lightly resting here and there and stretching up into the azure blue of the vaulted heavens above.

Facing west is an old grey weather-worn gateway of colossal blocks of stone, the sculpturing on which has almost disappeared. From either side of this a massive colonnade of 84 columns with intervening trefoil-arched recesses is carried round to form a quadrangle about 250 feet long and 150 feet broad.

These fine cloisters and the temple they contain, with their fluted pillars, definitely proportioned bases, Doric capitals, massive square architraves to the doors and elegant trefoiled arches, although sadly ruined, still show all the characteristics of the old classical Kashmiri style of architecture.

From a mound in the quadrangle rises what was originally a lofty central edifice approached by a wide flight of steps. The ruins of the temple are now only 40 feet in height. Each of the four sides is surmounted by very beautiful and graceful trefoiled arches. From the western entrance we look down a nave with sculptured walls, through the choir, to the cella or sanctuary. And on either side of the nave flanking the central building there are two side chapels.

If the original roof was of the same character as that found on other temples of that period, which still remain, there may have been a lofty pyramid of stone blocks towering up to a pinnacle 75 feet above the ground and flanked by smaller pyramids covering the wings on either side.

From the Rájatarangini, the famous chronicles of Kashmir, it appears probable that the central temple was built by Ranaditya about the first half of the fifth century A.D., and the colonnade by King Lalatáditya in the eighth century.

Kashmir has changed less than most countries as the centuries roll on, and it is not difficult to picture to ourselves the olden days—the temple of Martand bathed in the rosy glow of the sinking sun. On the steps of the central edifice, at its western portal, stands the Hindu priest blowing his shell trumpet, while another strikes a bell. A few figures clad in grey woollen tunics and caps are moving about. At the edge of a neighbouring tank are women filling their brass water-pots. And all the surroundings, the mountains and valley, the plateau stretching away to Anant Nág and the distant encircling ranges, silhouetted in purple against the golden sky, are the same as now. And as night falls there is wafted on the still air the fragrant odour of incense and the sound of voices chanting in the temple under that pyramidal roof which rises as a great shadow pointing to the starry firmament above.

CHAPTER II

HISTORICAL EPOCHS

Early Hindu—Buddhist—Hindu Kings—Tribal Wars—Tartar Invasion—Mohammedan Rule—Kashmir Sultans—The Moghuls—Akhbar—Jehangir—Afghan Tyranny—Sikh Invasion—Ceded to British—Transferred to Dogra Dynasty.

THE Kashmiris owe much of their character and disposition to their environment and especially to a long history of tyranny and oppression.

Nothing is known of the early ages when aboriginal tribes dwelt on the shores of the great Kashmir lake or in the recesses of the dense forests. The earliest legends are Hindu. But when or how that cult was introduced we know not.

In olden days there used to be several books of chronicles of the kings of Kashmir. These histories were called Rája-tarangini, and it is said that there were as many as fifteen. Early in the fourteenth century most of the old Hindu books were destroyed by Zulzu the Tartar invader, and the work of destruction was later on completed by Sikander the Iconoclast. In the following century the enlightened King Zain-ul-ab-ul-Din instituted a search for ancient manuscripts; and copies of four of the books were found. Of these Kalhana's Chronicles were by far the most important. But the history of thirty-five of the early Hindu kings was still missing. Subsequently an old manuscript was discovered written on birch bark. This was called the Ratnákar Purana and was of especial interest, as it contained a record of those kings whose reigns were omitted from Kalhana's history. Zain-ul-ab-ul-Din had a Persian translation made. But both this and the original have disappeared. A copy of the translation is, however, said to have been obtained by

Hassan, who wrote a History of Kashmir in Persian. From this and the Chronicles of Kalhana it appears that there was a succession of Kashmir kings from 3120 B.C. to 1445 B.C. Of the numerous dynasties the Pándava is perhaps the best known. It is said that Ramadeo, the second of this line, founded a large city on the Martand plateau and built the first temple there. And another, King Sandimán, (2629-2564 B.C.) is stated to have built an extensive city on the site now occupied by the Wular Lake. He is also said to have built the original Jyeshteswara temple upon the hill now known as the Takht-i-Suleiman.

Many Kashmiri Hindus hold that the present temples of Martand on the Takht and elsewhere were built by a race of giants or gods, and they triumphantly ask whether any human beings could construct such massive edifices.

The earliest coins which have been found in Kashmir are those of Avanti Varma of the Utpala dynasty (875 A.D.). And it was this king who erected the temple of Avantipoor, which is similar in construction to that of Martand. But there is an immense gap between this period and the early kings of Kashmir legend.

We cannot even tell how long it was before Buddhism first made its appearance. But we know that 250 years before the Christian era, Asoka, the great Buddhist King of Northern India, also held sway over Kashmir. And Buddhism was then the national religion. The ancient capital of Kashmir, the ruins of which can still be seen extending along the foot of the Zabrwan Mountain from Pandretthan to Aitgaji gap, is said to have been founded by him. And throughout the valley many stupas and temples were erected in his reign. His son Jaloka is, however, said to have reverted to the worship of Siva, on account of his attachment to the Nága maidens.

A subsequent revival of Buddhism took place, and that religion reached its zenith in Kashmir in the time of King Kanishka, the Indo-Scythian monarch of northern extraction, who reigned about 40 A.D., the time when in the west our own isles were being invaded by the Romans.

The famous third great council of Buddhism was held at this period. And the proceedings of the synod, engraven on copper plates, were, according to the Chinese pilgrim Hwen Thseng, deposited in a stupa at a place which has been identified as Ushkpur, near Baramula. In 1882 Mr Garrick, of the Archæological Survey, carried out very extensive excavations in hope of finding them, but failed. The success of recent explorations in the north of India encourage us to hope that they may yet be discovered.

Buddhism gradually declined and by 638 A.D. it is recorded that the monasteries were few and partly deserted and the people addicted to Devas.[1] The Buddhists were then leaving Kashmir and gradually making their way eastward into Tibet and across the Chinese Empire.

For a lengthy period Kashmir was now again ruled by a succession of Hindu kings, some of whom were tributary to China. Of the disposition of one Mihirakula (515 A.D.) we obtain a glimpse. South of Aliabad Serai, where the Pir Panjal route to the Punjab emerges from Kashmir, there is a ridge called the Hasti Vanj. A legend relates how the king, who was marching his army across, was so amused by the cries, struggles and agonies of an elephant which had fallen down the ravine that he ordered a hundred more to be forced over the precipice.[2]

Lalatáditya, who reigned from 697-738 A.D., is the best known of the Hindu kings. He built temples of which the most famous is Martand. He constructed canals, drained swamps and was a successful general. About a century later, 855-883 A.D., another famous king, Avanti Varma, also carried on drainage works and erected the Avantipoor temples. And his son Shankaravarman built the temples of Pattan.

[1] Hwen Thseng. Quoted by Dr Stein.
[2] Lawrence, *Valley of Kashmir*.

From this time dissensions and civil war began to arise and there were protracted periods of internecine strife. Kashmir clans, the descendants of which still exist in the valley, Dámaras, Pálas, Khashas, Tántris and Thakkurs, formed predatory bands and carried fire and the sword throughout the country. Demoralization followed. And in 1305 A.D., in the reign of King Simha Deva, Kashmir is said to have been a country of drunkards, gamblers and profligate women.

Then came the Tartar Invasion. Srinagar was burnt and the population massacred or carried off as slaves. But Zulzu, the invader, was forced by famine to retreat, and with his whole force and thousands of unhappy captives he perished in the snow on one of the southern passes.

With a short interruption of fifteen years Kashmir in 1323 A.D. came for nearly four and a half centuries under Mohammedan rule. First a Tibetan adventurer, Rainchan Shah, who for political reasons embraced Islam, and then the Kashmiri Mohammedan dynasty, came into power. Of the Kashmiri Moslem Kings, Sikander the Iconoclast (1394 A.D.) is best known, as his reign was one of terror and marked by the demolition of the magnificent old Hindu temples and the slaughter of thousands of Hindus. Many others fled and most, especially those of the lower castes, embraced Mohammedanism.

The most famous of the Kashmiri Sultans was Zain-ul-ab-ul-Din, who reigned for fifty-two years from 1417 A.D. He ruled well and carried out many works of public utility, and his reign was perhaps the happiest period in Kashmir history. His son was a drunkard and chaos supervened.

After sustaining one serious defeat the troops of the Emperor Akbar reached Srinagar in 1586 A.D. A battle took place at the foot of the Takht-i-Suleiman. This was not decisive. But after more fighting the Moghuls were eventually victorious. Akbar built the great bastioned wall round the Hari Parbat Hill. Jehangir, who succeeded

Akbar, has left his mark in Kashmir in numerous gardens with chenar trees and fountains.

During the Moghul rule, Kashmir was, on the whole, prosperous and fertile and the shawl industry first assumed importance.

As the Moghul empire began to wane the local governors of Kashmir became increasingly tyrannical and oppressive, especially to the Hindus. But the Afghan rule from 1752-54 is regarded as the worst period of Kashmir history.

We read of Hindus being tied up two and two in grass sacks and thrown into the Dal Lake. They were not allowed to wear shoes or turbans. A poll-tax was instituted. And once again the alternatives were set before them, of conversion, death or flight. The abduction of Hindu women, too, by the dissolute Mussulman rulers was common.

At last a measure of relief came. In 1819, in response to an appeal from Kashmir, Ranjit Singh the Sikh, " Lion of the Punjab," sent in a force which defeated the governor of Kashmir near Shupeyon. This change of rule, although an improvement, benefited the Hindus more than the Mussulmans. Moorcroft, speaking of those days, refers to the deserted condition of villages, and to the exorbitant *taxes*, amounting sometimes to nine-tenths of the whole harvest. And he says: " The Sikhs seem to look upon the Kashmirians as little better than cattle. The murder of a native by a Sikh is punished by a fine to the Government of from sixteen to twenty rupees, of which four rupees are paid to the family of the deceased, if a Hindu, and two rupees if he was a Mohammedan." Unpaid forced labour was the rule, and for this purpose people were seized and driven along the roads, tied together with rope, like slave gangs. Moti Ram, the first Sikh governor, however, introduced a more humane régime. But his successors were incompetent. The combined effect of their feeble administration, a severe earthquake in 1827 and famine in 1831 was to reduce Kashmir once more to the depths of distress. An able governor,

Mian Singh, restored prosperity to some extent. But after his assassination by mutinous troops, disorder and anarchy became universal. Meanwhile Rajah Gulab Singh, the Dogra ruler of Jammu, had twice entered Kashmir. The first time was in 1819 with the Sikh force sent by Ranjit Singh. On the second occasion, in 1842, he came in to restore order after the murder of Mian Singh.

On 9th March 1846, in the treaty following the Battle of Sobraon, Kashmir was ceded to the British Government by the Sikhs in lieu of a war indemnity. And a week later, on 16th March, the British transferred Kashmir to Golab Singh, receiving in exchange 75 lakhs of rupees (£500,000, less than one year's revenue at the present time), and the promise of a nominal annual tribute, one horse, twelve shawl goats and three pairs of Kashmir shawls. Golab Singh engaged to " join with the whole of his military force the British troops when employed within the hills, or in the territories adjoining his possessions; and the British Government promised " to give its aid to Maharajah Golab Singh in protecting his territories from external enemies."

The British had at once to fulfil their part of the treaty, for Imamuddin, the Governor of Kashmir, refused to give up Kashmir and defeated the troops sent by Maharajah Golab Singh to turn him out. On the movement, however, of a British force into Jammu territory, he surrendered. Maharajah Golab Singh was a stern and vigorous but capable and just ruler. He came to Kashmir and himself took charge of the administration, to the great benefit of the State. He died in 1857.

Maharajah Ranbir Singh, his third son, who succeeded him, was a just and tolerant ruler and a good friend to the British in the dark days of the Mutiny. But during his reign Kashmir, although its condition was improving, again suffered much at the hands of rapacious officials, who took advantage of the absence of the Maharajah in Jammu.

This brief review of its history shows that for centuries

Kashmir was subject to constant changes of administration, that good rulers were rare and there was no permanency in the system of government. And although such cruelty as that of the Afghans was the exception, still there were long periods when religious persecution was rife, and tyranny, oppression, exaction and virtual slavery at the hands of the rulers, alternated with anarchy, disorder and even civil war.

Then came the Pax Britannica, Dogra rule but under Christian influence. Hindus, Buddhists, Kashmiri Mohammedans, Moghuls, Afghans and Sikhs had all in turn occupied this unhappy country. But with the accession of Maharajah Golab Singh dawned an era of peace, continuity of administration, reform and development of the resources of the country.

In half a century Kashmir has, under Dogra rule, progressed far upon the road to recovery from its sorrows and woes. Time is still required.

The habits and customs of generations become a second nature and are slow in passing away. It may be long before we have complete religious toleration in Kashmir. But education and reform of all kinds are steadily advancing, and freedom cannot be far behind.

CHAPTER III

THE PEOPLE

Character—Food—Women—Religion—Shrine Worship—Hindus—Clans—Language—Proverbs—A Dialogue.

THE two indispensable officials of the Kashmir village are the lumbardar and the chowkidar. The latter is practically the village policeman, and his duties are light, as although the Kashmiri is by nature deceitful and given to petty larceny, in the villages there is a public opinion which compels the fulfilment of pecuniary engagements or contracts and puts down fraud and dishonesty. This system works fairly satisfactorily, so far as the village is concerned, but there are, of course, frequent defaulters. In relation to Government, the Kashmiri conscience is very lax, and deceit and robbery are condoned by the villagers even if they do not aid and abet. Europeans are treated as if they were officials, so they have to be careful or they will be cheated. Indeed, they have suffered much in connection with the grain trade. Large advances made to villagers in connection with contracts for grain delivery have been absolutely repudiated and the money misappropriated. And hitherto, in matters of this kind, European capitalists have received no encouragement from the Kashmiri Government, and have sometimes been unable to obtain justice.

The Kashmiri lumbardar, or village headman, is usually an elderly man, often tall, with a beard dyed red with henna, with his upper lip closely cropped and a large rather dirty white turban on his shaven head. He has a long tunic or pheran of puttoo (Kashmiri woollen cloth), wide, baggy cotton trousers, cut off just below the knee, bare legs and feet, with putties and stout, pointed shoes.

The ordinary villager looks very dirty. On his head he wears a greasy old grey, orange or red skull-cap. His cotton pheran, rather like a night-gown, but with wide sleeves, originally white, is now grey. Loose, short cotton trousers and plaited sandals of rice straw complete his costume. But on his back he has a long, grey woollen Kashmiri blanket, with the end thrown over his left shoulder. Those who have Government employment or service with Europeans often wear puttoo coats, putties and leather sandals (Plate 6).

Many Kashmiris wear charms. The little children have them sewn on to the tops of their caps, a smooth polished pebble, two or three leopard's claws or a metal ornament. The men and women have little oblong packets, about two inches by one, of cloth or leather, tied to their caps or round the neck or one of the arms. These amulets usually contain a piece of paper inscribed with cabalistic signs or with a few words from the Koran. The people are good-tempered, often merry; they have a distinct sense of humour and enjoy a joke. Sir Walter Lawrence gives a typical instance of their grim humour. " One day while hearing a petition I noticed an elderly Hindu villager standing on his head. He remained in that position for nearly half an hour, when I asked him his business. He then explained that his affairs were in so confused a state that he did not know whether he was standing on his head or his heels." If making a petition, a common demonstration to indicate their sad condition is " a procession of two men and one woman. One man wears a shirt of matting. One carries a pan of embers on his head, and the woman bears a number of broken earthen pots." They are, however, patient, industrious in their field occupations and capable of great endurance.

The Kashmiri coolie is a wonderful being. In these days of revived athletic cult a meed of praise should not be withheld from men who can carry a weight of 100 lb. for five or

6. GROUP OF KASHMIRI VILLAGERS AND CHILDREN.

more miles, and who often carry a load of 60 lb. for a whole march of six kos (12 miles).

They begin early. Little children may often be seen coming down from the forest, each carrying a load of wood proportioned to his size. A little five-year-old child is carrying a bundle of sticks weighing at least 30 lb. Behind him are two or three boys, perhaps eight or ten years old, each with faggots of wood from 40 to 60 lb. in weight.

In their daily life the villagers, who are mostly cultivators, are in the habit of carrying heavy loads of grass and other field produce.

In appearance the coolie is often sallow, about 5 feet 6 in height, with a short beard and shaven head, covered with a dirty skull-cap. His physique is not at first sight impressive. He is spare. There is no great obvious development of muscle, certainly nothing of the "Sandow" type. But the muscle is there, hard and compact and able to perform these astonishing feats of load-carrying.

The coolie is in many ways deft with his hands. He can twist saplings into tough withes for lashing together loose bundles. He can plait most serviceable grass sandals and prove himself an agricultural "handy man" in many directions. Nevertheless, he is timid, afraid of bogeys and of being left alone in the dark. Most coolies are cowardly and inclined to be untruthful and deceitful, but not all. I have known brave men who have risked their lives for others, with no applauding gallery and no laudatory press to approve. Kashmiri coolies sometimes deserve decorations—but instead they too often get blows and curses, not often from their English employers, but very frequently from the native servants or chaprasies of Europeans.

The coolie is often of cheerful disposition. If during the day he grumbles at the weight of his load, the length of the road or the steepness of the hills and the probability that the camping place may be cold and without shelter or firewood, he soon forgets his woes when the tents are pitched, fires lighted and his rice is cooking in a large earthenware pot, from which issues a savoury smell. And when he has eaten his fill he often breaks out into song as he sits by the camp-fire, and becomes conversational and even confidential.

Ah, those camp-fires! What pleasant associations they conjure up, as after the toil of the day one sits and watches the mighty sheets of flame tongued and forked, twisting, bending, leaping, flashing or even fiercely roaring and compelling one to shift one's seat. In the background the tall, dark shadowy outline of the firs or the grey rocks catching up and reflecting back the ruddy glow, while showers of sparks like golden rain are given off and floating upwards are lost in the darkness above. The aromatic scent of the burning firewood is carried on the crisp, cold, pure mountain air. A little further off is another similar fire, casting its red light on the faces of the cook and some of his coolie helpers. No sound is heard but the crackling of wood and the occasional louder explosion of a noisy fragment, the call of a fox or jackal close by or the croak of the night-jar.

How often have we sat by similar camp-fires in years gone by with many different companions, some of whom have passed away.

In spite of his great physical strength and powers of endurance, the Kashmiri is highly strung and neurotic, and he will often weep on slight provocation. In the presence of very little danger he will sob like a child. These people can bear pain much better than Europeans, but owing to want of self-control they make more fuss. Naturally impulsive and huffy, they respond readily to tactful handling. On the whole they are grateful for benefits. Their moral sense is fairly well developed. They readily distinguish between right and wrong. In money affairs they are close, and the more wealthy are mean. They spend little, and except at weddings care nothing for show. Even the rich wear dirty clothes lest they should be thought too well off. They are affectionate

Photo by] [*G. W. Possnet.*

7. KASHMIRI PEASANT HOLDING A "KANGRI."

Photo by] [*R. E. Shorter.*

8. KASHMIRI GIRL.

in family life, and very good in nursing sick relatives (Plate 7).

The staple food in the valley is rice. Round the hills it is maize and wheat, and higher up buckwheat and barley. Vegetables and lentils, peas, etc., are largely consumed. Meat is a luxury for occasional consumption. A man doing full work will eat as much as 3 lb. of rice in a day.

Kashmiri children are often bright, pleasant and pretty, but spoilt. Owing to the conditions of life, they acquire, in certain directions, a remarkable gift of bearing responsibility and even of taking initiative action. A small child, five years old, will be seen driving an enormous buffalo along and thumping it with a big stick at intervals. Children will cleverly round up sheep and goats, for there are no properly-trained sheep-dogs. Early in the morning they take the herds and flocks up to the hills and drive them back at night. And often we may see a very small child lying on the grass by the side of a babbling stream, in entire charge of the flocks and herds which are peacefully grazing around. The girls are the great water-carriers. Owing to hard work they soon lose their good looks. They are married at an early age, soon after ten. Little girls wear small skull-caps, and may have their hair beautifully done in a large number of plaits spread out over the back and gracefully braided together (Plate 8). After marriage, however, a thicker turban-like red cap, studded with pins, is worn, and over it a square of country cloth to act as a veil and cover the whole back. The rest of the usual dress of the village women is an ample pheran of dark blue cotton print, with a red pattern stamped on it; or the gown may be of grey striped cotton or wool, with wide sleeves turned back and showing a dirty lining. Round the neck a collar of silver or brass, enamelled in red or blue, or a coral and silver bead necklace, is usually worn; and large metal ear-rings are common. Glass bangles or massive silver bracelets and finger rings, with agate or cornelian, complete the list of ordinary jewellery worn by

Kashmiri women. The feet are bare, or leather shoes, often green, are worn. The houses are without chimneys, so the inmates become smoke-begrimed. There are fewer Mohammedan women than men. The ratio is about nine to ten. Perhaps for this reason polygamy is comparatively uncommon.

More females are born than males, but baby girls do not receive so much care as the boys, and the mortality from smallpox and infantine diseases is higher. The girls are often mothers at the age of fourteen.

Kashmiri women vary very much. A very large number of the peasant women are dirty, degraded and debased. But there are not a few who are very different and who are capable and manage their houses and children and even their husbands.

Kashmiris are attached to their own country and often use the proverb—*Tsari chhu kand thari peth qarar*—"A sparrow is content on its own branch."

About five per cent. of the Mohammedans are Shiahs. Although a highly respectable community, these are looked upon by the orthodox Mussulmans as outcasts. Curiously enough, although the Sunnis are friendly with the Hindus, the Shiahs abhor them. The Shiahs are more friendly to Christians than ordinary Mohammedans. They may be recognized by their turbans, which are tied differently. Apart from shrine worship and times of special stress from disease or disaster, the Kashmiris show very little religious zeal or earnestness.

They are called Pir-parast, *i.e.*, saint worshippers. "No man will dare to pass a shrine on horseback, and I once saw a striking example of the danger of neglecting this rule. A marriage-party was crossing a stream, above which stood the shrine of a saint. All of them dismounted and passed over the bridge, but the father of the bridegroom, with the bridegroom in his arms, rode boldly over. The bridge broke, and the horse, father and son were precipitated into the stream, where they lay struggling. I ran up and rebuked the crowd for not assisting the sufferers, but they looked

Photo by] [*R. E. Shorter.*

9. FAIR AT HAZRAT BAL ZIARUT.

on gloomily and said the man richly deserved his fate. After some trouble I induced some of my own people to disentangle the men from the horse, and then one of the attendants of the shrine explained to me that within the last ten years four men who had despised the saint and had ridden over the bridge had been killed." [1]

After the Hazrat Bal ziarut the shrine at Tsrar ranks as the most sacred. Indeed, a pilgrimage thither is supposed to obviate any special necessity for going to Mecca. In case of famine, earthquake, or cholera, thousands of people resort to Tsrar, most of them bringing offerings with them—rice, walnuts, money, a fat capon, or even a ram. Twice or thrice a year, under ordinary conditions, large fairs are held at the more important of the shrines (Plate 9). Thousands gather together: the roads are lined with temporary booths with a great display of sweetmeats and cakes, painted clay figures, fruit and ornaments such as ear-rings, glass bangles, metal bracelets, bright-coloured skull-caps and waistcoats. Large numbers of women attend. For them it is the equivalent of the Bank Holiday. Here too may be seen the Kashmiri minstrels. These have long clarionet-like pipes and drums and produce most weird music, often in the minor key. Sometimes they are reinforced by fiddles—curious instruments, with a barbaric twang. Such companies of strolling musicians often have with them dancing boys with long hair, dressed up as women. As a general rule these people are Mussulmans. They are in special request at weddings and harvest feasts. Some of them are said to be good actors and to have valuable dresses and stage properties.

Among the more important shrines of the second rank may be mentioned that of Zain Shah at Eishmakám, which is much resorted to by boatmen, who offer up there the first locks of hair of their children. The Kulgám ziarut, with its pagoda-like roof, its painted lattice work and rich carving,

[1] Lawrence, *Valley of Kashmir.*

is noteworthy. But many of the larger villages have very handsome ziaruts, most of which stand in impressive groves of Kabuli poplar, elm, chenar, or of the rounded dark green foliaged Celtis Australensis.

In the ranks of those who were converted from Hinduism there were two whose names are now regarded with great reverence. One of these is Makhdum Sahib, whose shrine is on the Hari Parbat hill, and the other Sheikh Nur Din, whose memorial is the shrine at Tsrar. These two names are constantly invoked by Kashmiris in times of trouble.

Sheikh Nur Din is the great national saint of Kashmir. He had ninety-nine disciples or khalifas. Most of the best-known shrines can be traced back to one or other of these, as, for instance, the ziaruts at Shukr-ud-din, Eishmakám, Bába Marishi and Poshkar.

The successors of the khalifas were called Rishis, and some of the Pirs still bear that title.

There are about 65,000 Brahmans in Kashmir. Nearly half of these live in the city or larger towns. They are divided up into clans and families, with distinctive names, and intermarriage is not permitted within the clan.

The Hindus of Kashmir are not nearly so particular about caste observances as those in India. They will, for instance, drink water which is brought by a Mussulman, and eat food which has been cooked on the boat of a Mohammedan, and will even allow Mussulmani foster-mothers for their infants. On the other hand, curiously enough, they refuse to eat fruit of a red colour, such as rosy apples and tomatoes.

The Brahmans have faces of the pure high Arian type. The Mohammedans have well-shaped heads, with good broad and high forehead. The nose is rather prominent and tends to be hooked, especially in the older people. The upper lip is rather deep. The average height of the Kashmiri is about five feet four inches to eight inches. It is commoner to find them below than above this. Their muscular development is good, especially the chest and arms. The legs are often rather thin and spindle-shaped.

Among the Mussulmans there are also clans, but these are only nominal; and there are no restrictions placed upon intermarriage except with Saiyads at the top of the social scale and menials at the bottom.

There are still in the valley many families of the Chak clan, but they have settled down into quiet and peaceable cultivators. It was not always so. In the reign of Sultan Zain-ul-ab-ul-Din they gave much trouble and formed bands of marauders. It is thought that they came from some district to the north of Kashmir, and that perhaps they were originally Dards. At the north-west end of the valley there are the ruins of an old Chak city. And the beautiful Tregám pool, where a clear stream issues from the limestone rock, is believed to have been enclosed by Maddan Chak. In 1556 A.D. Ghazi Khan, son of Kazi Chak, was *de facto* ruler in Kashmir. And it was the Chaks under Yakub Khan and Shams-i-Chak who defeated the Emperor Akbar's forces at their first invasion of Kashmir; and they were again very nearly successful in repelling the second invasion in 1586.

There are still some Pathán colonies at the north-west end of Kashmir. Of these perhaps the most interesting is a clan of Afridis, who live in a valley opening into the Lolab. They are differently dressed to the Kashmiris and more manly, and with their long matchlocks, swords and shields they make a brave show.

Another clan, of lower class than the Chaks, and, like most of the inferior class in Kashmir, with darker complexions than the ordinary cultivators, is that of the Galawáns. These gave great trouble during the Pathán reign. They drove off flocks and herds, looted granaries and even attacked wedding parties and abducted the bride. Being well-armed and all mounted, they eluded pursuit, and it was not till

Colonel Mian Singh, in the days of the Sikhs, captured and hanged the chief and exterminated a large part of the tribe that their depredations ceased. The rest were deported to Bunji, on the Gilgit road. Many, however, have returned, and horse-stealing is still not uncommon.

The lowest class in Kashmir is that of the sweepers or wátuls. These are extremely dishonest. Many of them are cobblers, others work in leather and straw or act as house and road sweepers. They are dark skinned and are really the gipsies of Kashmir. Their women are often quite beautiful. Those who are more settled live in little Kashmir houses. Others dwell in clusters of wattle huts, with rounded tops, perched by preference upon slightly raised ground. Some of them are eaters of carrion, and these are treated as outcasts by the Mohammedan peasantry.

Although ruled by Hindus, Kashmir is now really a Mohammedan country. For ninety-three per cent. of the people are Mussulmans. There are few Hindu cultivators, but in the villages there are many shopkeepers and subordinate revenue and forest officers of this religion. More than half of the Hindu population, however, lives in Srinagar.

The language is of Hindu origin with Sanskrit roots and allied to Western Punjabi. As may be supposed it is rich in agricultural terms. But the vocabulary is small and inadequate for present day use, being conspicuously weak in terms both for the implements and materials of modern civilized life and for abstract ideas.

With the exception of the Rájatarangini, chronicles of the kings of Kashmir, some Hindu sacred literature and a few lives of Rishis or saints, there is no indigenous literature. The people are profoundly illiterate. Those who can read usually prefer Persian or Urdu to Kashmiri. In the district we sometimes find only three or four in a whole village who can read, and these usually belong to the official or priestly classes.

Kashmiri is a curious mixed language. Originally, in

the days of the Hindu kings, it was doubtless to a large extent derived from Sanskrit. But the many political changes, with their introduction of Mohammedan rulers for long periods, account for the large number of Persian and Arabic words which have become incorporated. At the present time perhaps three-quarters of the vocabulary is derived from Urdu, Persian and Arabic sources, and the remainder from Sanskrit. But undoubtedly the purer the Kashmiri the larger is the proportion of words of Sanskrit derivation. There are many interesting and amusing proverbs in frequent use by the people. Some of these give an insight into the views of the people with regard to their rulers, their religious teachers, and their own village life. Not a few of them breathe out memories of their unhappy history and the oppression which they have suffered for such long periods. For instance—

"Hakímas ta hákimas nishih rachhtam Khodayo."

"O God, save me from physicians and rulers"—

is pungent, but justified by almost daily experience in the East.

"Pir na bod yakin bod."

"The pir is not great. It is credulity which is great."

This shows that in spite of the almost universal respect which is paid to the Pirs or saints, it is nevertheless fully recognized that they make great demands on the credulity of their followers.

In Kashmir, influence is often of far more value than money, because it is the source of money. This is emphasized in the following proverb—

"Kanh mat ditam
Kantil nitam."

"Don't give me anything, but listen to me."

Mohammedans are often said to present some of the characters of the Pharisees of old. That this opinion is endorsed by some at least of the Kashmiris, so far as their priests are concerned, the following proverb shows—

"Yih moullah dapi ti gatshi karun, yih moullah kari ti gatshi na karun.

"Do as the priest says but not as he does."

Some of the proverbs enunciate sound principles in a terse phrase, *e.g.*—

"Manz atsun chhu kanz atsun."

"To go between, *i.e.*, to act as a surety, is to put your head into a mortar."

"Khairas tájíl ta nyáyas tátil."

"Swift to do good, slow to do evil."

Similar to our proverb, "Wolf in sheep's clothing," is the Kashmiri *Gabi buthi ramahun*, "A wolf with the face of a sheep." In his dictionary of Kashmiri proverbs and sayings, the Rev. J. Hinton Knowles has gathered together a large number of similar epigrams from the interesting folklore of the valley.

The administration of justice is still most unsatisfactory. The highest magistrates are upright and uncorrupt. But the police system is a scandal and disgrace. The people regard the police in much the same light as they do earthquakes, famine or pestilence—as a calamity. A well-known Kashmiri proverb illustrates this well. *Khuda sanz khar, tah naid sanz chep*. This means, "God gives the scaldhead, but the barber makes matters worse by wounding your head." This proverb is said to be often applied to a woman who, having lost a child in the river, is arrested by the police on a trumped-up charge of murder. False charges of this kind are extremely common. I remember being told of two men who were attacked by a bear and one of them was killed. The other was promptly arrested by the police and not released until he had paid a substantial sum. In police inquiries the innocent usually suffer quite as much as the guilty, and the giving and taking of bribes is shameless and notorious. Except where the evidence is unusually strong, it is almost impossible to secure a conviction, in cases in which the accused is a man of means. The whole police force needs radical reform. And to effect this it ought to have European officers until a reliable local staff has been trained.

It is rare now to find a village of any size in which there are no old patients of the Kashmir Mission Hospital. What is their attitude towards the Institution? It may be depicted in an imaginary conversation, which we will suppose to be held under a chenar tree near the village tank. Those who take part in it are—Ramzana, a villager; Mohammed Sheikh, headman of village; Lachman Pandit, a Hindu shopkeeper; and Maulvi Nur-ud-Din, Mohammedan priest.

Ramzana (entering his village after having been in the Mission Hospital for disease of the bone of his right leg for two months). How are you all?

Mohammed Sheikh. Quite well, thank God. How are you? they did not cut off your leg then!

Ramzana. No. I thought they were going to and tried to run away, but they caught hold of me, and before I knew where I was they had put me on a table, tied a bandage above my knee and given me some curious stuff to smell. I know I struggled, but soon everything began to whirl round and round, and then I do not remember anything more till I found myself in a very large room, in a comfortable bed, with a red blanket and white sheets and a floor shining like glass. On either side of me and opposite there were rows of beds full of men and boys, who all seemed as jolly as anything.

Mohammed Sheikh. Yes, I know. I went there with Farzi, you know, my little granddaughter. There *was* a crowd in the room where we had to wait for two hours before we could see the doctor. He came in to see us at the beginning, and read some verses out of the Holy Gospel, and then told us what the meaning was, and he talked Kashmiri just like a book. Farzi was quite blind and they did something to her eyes. They did not give her anything on a towel to smell, but dropped something into her eyes and then they put in what looked like a needle. The funny thing was that it did not seem to hurt. Farzi never said a word. And the doctor held up two fingers and said, "How many are there?" and I was absolutely astounded to hear her say "two." The wisdom (hikmat) of these foreigners is wonderful. And they have very gentle hands. Then they took Farzi and put her into a women's ward, where there were several other little girls, and there was a miss sahib, who was so kind and gave the children dolls and toys and they had a curious box which you could wind up like a clock and it then produced music like I once heard played at the Palace, where His Highness the Maharajah Sahib Bahadur lives. And the miss sahib used to come every day and read from the Holy Gospel about the Spirit of God, the Holy Jesus, Who was sinless and went about doing good, and Who died to take away our sins.

Ramzana. Why, that was just what the doctor sahib did at our end of the hospital, and we had great discussions when he went away. One man there, an old fakir, said that he had travelled in many countries and been to Africa too, and that lots of the English were bad and violent and drank too much and used dreadful language. But that he had found out that those who did this did not believe in their own religion and hated the name of Jesus, and that those who were disciples of the Holy Jesus were quite different. And he told us about an old colonel sahib who had been very good to him, and he said, "Since I met him I believe in Christ and mean to obey His words."

Maulvi Nur-ud-Din. There is no God but God, and Mohammed is the Prophet of God. (Other villagers join in repeating the Mohammedan Kalima.) Maulvi Nur-ud-Din. These foreigners have a Book and they believe in God, in a way, but they do not acknowledge the Prophet Mohammed, and their Scriptures are tampered with and spoiled, and they say that Hazrat Isa was God Incarnate, which is rank heresy.

Mohammed Sheikh. I don't know. I remember the miss sahib used to tell us that you could tell a tree by its fruits, and she said the Christians led purer and holier lives than the Mussulmans, owing to the fact that they believe in Christ and He helps them.

Ramzana. That was just what the doctor sahib said.

Lachman Pandit. You Mohammedans think you are the only people who believe in one God, but we Hindus do, and our poet Tulsi Das has taught us that God is one and our Father, and He is all powerful. Why should He not be able to become incarnate as the Christians say He did? I, too, was in the Mission Hospital twenty years ago, when I broke my leg, and I shall always remember the teaching I heard there and the care which I received, far more than I had had from my own people. I would long ago have liked to become a Christian, believing that religion to be the purest of all and the most full of hope and love. In it I see the fulfilment of much which the best and noblest Hindus have striven after. But I dare not. I should become an outcast and lose all that makes life worth having.

Mohammed Sheikh. Quite right, Panditji. Every one should stick to his own religion. If God had meant you to be a Christian, He would have made you one.

Maulvi Nur-ud-Din. No, no. There is only one true religion, "La Illahu illah Allah." But I admit that if all Christians were like those at the Mission Hospital, we could live with them on brotherly terms. My father died three years ago. I hated the idea of his dying under an unbeliever's roof. And yet the old man died quite happy. He was a true Mussulman, but he had a very special reverence for Hazrat Isa.

Ramzana. That's just it. Nearly all the people seem to learn that there. When the doctor sahib was reading prayers in the ward, at least ten people joined in, saying Amen fervently. Now there is Lassoo. He is quite different since he was there. I am sure he does not tell nearly so many lies, and he no longer beats his womenfolk. I believe he has a copy of the Gospels in his house.

Maulvi Nur-ud-Din. He had better mind what he is about or I will have him excommunicated. Tell him to bring the book to me. But it is time for prayers. Run and tell Rasula to call the faithful.

(They all walk away slowly, except the Pandit, who goes down to the stream to fill his brass lota.)

Photo by] [*R. E. Shorter.*

10. THE MAR CANAL.

CHAPTER IV

SRINAGAR

Population—Bridges—Palace—H.H. the Maharajah—Administration —Merchants—Silk Factory—On the River—Shah-i-Hamadán Mosque—Sikhs—Hindus—Street Life.

SRINAGAR was built about 960 A.D. Its population now is approximately 126,344. So crowded are the houses, however, that the total area of the city does not exceed six square miles, and within this space there are at least 20,000 houses, occupied by, on an average, six people each. It is not therefore surprising that the conditions of life should be extremely insanitary.

The city can be best seen by first passing down its great central highway, the river, and then traversing some of the chief streets and passing the Mar Canal. The latter is picturesque, with its overhanging buildings and rich tones of brown or light red in the woodwork, its quaint old bridges and irregular ghats (Plate 10).

The river as it passes through is about 200 feet wide. The current keeps the water comparatively fresh and clean. In its course through the city the Jhelum is spanned by seven bridges. The first of these, the Amira Kadal, or "bridge for the nobility," is just above the palace. The last bridge is the "bridge of departure," the Safr Kadal. The older of these bridges are extremely picturesque. They are entirely of wood. Immense beams, the trunks of unusually lofty cedars, are placed across the top of the piers. The latter are built of massive square trestles of deodar logs arranged in a square with the ends overlapping. The base of the pier rests on foundations of stone and piles driven in around.

The original method of placing the stones was to fill old boats with them, and to sink them at the required spot. The upper end of the pier is cantilevered in such a way as to diminish the span and the ends of the bridge are fixed down by alternate courses of stone and wood.

At one time two of the bridges had rows of shops on them, as some of those over the Mar Nalla still have (Plate 12). In some places, especially the Mar Canal, there is quite a reminiscence of Venice (Plate 10).

The palace of H.H. the Maharajah, known as the Sher Garhi, is an extensive building of a somewhat mixed style of architecture, but with an imposing façade rising from the water's edge and a pretty temple with a gilded roof. The gold and white, the coloured balconies and painted mouldings blend at a distance to form with the pale blue river and the light grey of distant mountains, a harmony of colour such as those which Turner loved to represent. In the palace there are some handsome darbar halls with painted ceilings. On the opposite side of the river is a broad flight of stone steps leading from the Basant Bagh to the river. From here in olden days a rope used to stretch to the palace, to which petitions were attached and hauled up by the palace officials for presentation to the Maharajah. The present Maharajah, Major-General Sir Pratab Singh, G.C.S.I., has reigned since 1885. Kashmir has been fortunate in having in him a ruler in sympathy with the needs of his subjects. While naturally conservative of the traditions and customs of orthodox Hinduism, he has pushed forward the cause of education, and has openly advocated its extension to females. On many occasions he has shown himself in favour of an enlightened and progressive policy (Plate 11). Deepest sympathy has been felt with His Highness in the great bereavements which he has sustained: the loss of his infant son, the heir to the throne, in 1905, and of his only surviving brother, who died in 1909. The late Rajah Sir Amar Singh was commander-in-chief and for some

Photo by] [*Clifton & Co.*

11. H.H. MAJOR-GENERAL SIR PRATAB SINGH, G.C.S.I., MAHARAJAH OF JAMMU AND KASHMIR.

years Vice-President of the State Council. His position was not an easy one. But he occupied it with conspicuous ability, and his early death was a very serious loss to the Kashmir State. His son, Prince Hari Singh, known as the Mian Sahib, is now the heir-apparent, and it is greatly hoped that he will carry on the best traditions of his distinguished family. The Government of Kashmir is comparatively simple. His Highness the Maharajah has a State Council consisting of Ministers for the chief departments—Revenue, Public Works, Home Affairs, Justice, etc. These ministers, able and distinguished men, have in turn as advisers, with executive powers, highly trained British officers lent by the Government of India. Thus there is a Settlement Commissioner, an ideal officer, Mr W. S. Talbot, who spends much of his time in the villages, personally supervising the work of the settlement; a Chief Engineer, Superintending Surgeon, Accountant-General, Conservator of Forests, and so on. The Governor of Kashmir is representative of H.H. the Maharajah and has full powers, with control over all matters relating to the collection of revenue, and he has authority over all the Tehsildars, the executive heads of the different Tehsils or districts.

There are few important public buildings in Kashmir. Above the first bridge, on the left bank, is the State Hospital, which was erected and ably organized by Dr A. Mitra, now Public Works Minister on the State Council. This hospital is excellently equipped and kept in beautiful order, and it is becoming increasingly useful. The Medical Department owes much to the administrative and professional capacity of successive Residency Surgeons, who have acted as Superintending Surgeons to the State Hospital, and among whom Colonel W. R. Edwards, C.M.G., should be specially mentioned. The present Indian Chief Medical Officer is Dr Mohun Lal. The Court of Justice opposite to the State Hospital is not an imposing building, and is hardly worthy of the able Chief Judge who presides there.

Further down on either side are the houses of the bankers, shawl merchants, silversmiths, embroiderers, and other merchants. Here may be seen beautiful specimens of Kashmir art — silver worked in delicate patterns of tracery, richly-carved walnut wood, *papier mâché* and embroidered goods of all kinds. The shawl trade, for which Kashmir used to be specially famous, has, however, to a large extent passed away. The industry received its death blow in the Franco-German War in 1870-71, after which the great demand in France ceased, and it has never really revived.

Its place has to some extent been taken by carpets, and in this branch, European firms, such as Messrs C. M. Hadow and W. Mitchell, compete successfully with local manufacturers, and put goods of excellent quality on the market.

One of the most successful of recent industrial enterprises in Kashmir is the revival of sericulture. It had been tried for many years and had failed from various causes, chief among which was the prevalence of diseased eggs. The industry was reorganized by the late Mr C. B. Walton, and his skill and experience changed the whole aspect of affairs and made it a brilliant success. Mr H. D. Douglas is now the capable director of the State silk factory, the largest in the world, with Mr M. MacNamara as second in command and an excellent staff of young Englishmen with more than 3300 employés. Last year over 260,000 lbs. of silk were produced. This is sold as yarn in Europe at an average of 16s. per lb. Some silk-weaving has been also done in the factory, but so far on a very small scale.

Up and down the river, boats are constantly plying. Many of these are small and, paddled by a crew of four smart men, they dash along with their one or two passengers. Occasionally we may see some notable person in a long boat with a central platform and red canopy and a numerous and brightly-attired crew, all paddling in good time—a pretty sight and in keeping with the surroundings. Presently an omnibus-boat passes us laden

[1] Resigned 1913.

Photo by] [*G. W. Millais*

12. BRIDGE OVER THE MAR NALLA.

with passengers and deep in the water. Or a large house-boat, of European pattern, with windows and upper-deck, comes steadily down-stream, carefully steered by men with large paddles and long punting poles.

The banks in many places are lined with great barge-like boats laden with stones, earth, hay, rice and many other cargoes. Where there is space on the sandy shore, lines of logs are moored and sawyers are busily at work with their double hand-saw, one standing on the beam, which is tilted up at an angle, and the other beneath.

Many of the houses which line the banks are built on stone foundations, among which are numerous carved fragments from demolished temples. In places, these walls are pierced by doorways leading to the water's edge. Above are balconies built out and resting on timber pillars or brackets. Some have windows of lattice work, beautifully pieced together. Here and there between the houses are alleys or lanes which open on to the river. And at such places there are often broad flights of rough stone steps. Here the scene is one of animation. At one corner a woman is seated washing clothes. The article is placed on a smooth stone and beaten with a short truncheon. The professional washermen swing the clothes against a stone. But owing to the splashing of dirty water, this is only permitted at certain appointed places. Another method is to tread the clothes in a line of basins hollowed out of a wooden log, the washermen holding meanwhile on to a railing.

Other women may be seen scouring their brass cooking-pots or filling large red globular earthen water-pots, and carrying them off on their heads. Here, too, there is colour, as the Hindu women often wear bright red, orange, violet and green pherans.

All around is the din of voices, for Kashmiris cannot work without making noise. Some, too, are quarrelling. The boatwomen, if roused, are most quarrelsome and vindictive. They will hurl abuse and vituperation at each other until they are absolutely hoarse with screaming. Not unfrequently a quarrel is then deliberately adjourned till the next day. Sometimes one of them ostentatiously inverts a rice basket. The next day, when it is turned up, the quarrel is recommenced and soon works up to the utmost pitch of intensity, only dying out as both sides become voiceless.

Close by, a gang of coolies is unshipping a cargo to the accompaniment of an antiphonal chant. Now, on our left, we see, standing well back from the water's edge, and approached by a broad impressive flight of steps, the simple form of a stately Hindu temple, with its lofty conical roof covered with silvery plates of shining metal and prolonged into a graceful, gilded pinnacle (Plate 13).

Further on we pass, on the right bank of the river, one of the most striking objects in the city, the Shah-i-Hamadán Mosque, which ranks after Hazrat Bal as the most sacred Mohammedan building in Kashmir. It is a massive square building, chiefly of timber, with carved eaves and balconies, tiers of grass and flower covered roof, and a very graceful central steeple, open below, and with four gables to it, and the spire carrying on its point a glittering crescent and golden ball (Plate 14).

Of the mosques, the Shah-i-Hamadán is the most important. It is the memorial of Mir Sayid Ali of Hamadán, who, in the days of the Kashmir Sultans, toward the end of the fourteenth century, exerted powerful influence in Kashmir. Indeed the forcible conversion of Kashmir to Mohammedanism is ascribed to his efforts, and those of his follower and successor, Mohammed Khan Hamadáni, who was associated with Sikander the Iconoclast in the great persecution which almost stamped out the Hindus. And further down on the right bank is a fine old grey stone mosque with a domed roof. This was built by the great Queen, Nur Mahal. It is now partly ruined and wholly picturesque. For many years it has been used as a granary; for the Mohammedans, despising the sex of the foundress, refuse to worship in it.

Photo by] *R. E. Shorter.*

13. ON THE RIVER, SRINAGAR.

The chief streets in Srinagar run parallel with the river on both sides. In the daytime they are crowded with a dense throng of pedestrians. We notice the number of Hindus with their foreheads and ears painted with red and yellow caste marks.

Here and there one or two Sikhs may be seen. The existence of the Sikh religion in Kashmir dates back at least to the time of the Moghuls. And both in the time of the Pathán rulers, and also when Ranjit Singh's force invaded Kashmir, it is said that the number of Sikhs was augmented. But the community is still quite small. Pursuing our way in the bazaar we notice many groups of school children carrying black wooden boards instead of slates. Most of them are Hindus.

When the Mussulman propaganda was being ruthlessly enforced, all the lower castes embraced Islam. So that the Hindus of Kashmir are almost all Brahmans, and they are usually called Pandits. Their intellectual superiority over the rest of the population must be admitted. They are quick of apprehension and have good memories. One of their besetting faults is conceit. But some of them are very superior, trustworthy, honest, clear-headed and industrious. A large number are officials in State employ. And many rise to positions of authority and responsibility. Most of the clerks in Government offices are Pandits. Others are merchants and shopkeepers. But they are not allowed to take up handicrafts such as carpentry, masonry, shoemaking and pottery. Neither are they allowed to become boatmen or porters.

In many respects they are the opposite of the Mohammedans. As a class, for instance, they are eager for education. The Mohammedans are grossly illiterate. And although there is a general similarity in dress, there are marked differences. The Hindu, unlike the Mussulman, wears a small turban of narrow cloth with the tuck on the right. He has narrow sleeves and tight trousers, and fastens his gown to the left. The Panditani (Hindu woman) affects garments of bright colours, red and orange being favourites, but her cap and head-dress are white, and she wears sandals and not leather shoes. Hindu women often have refined faces and gentle manners, and they are fairer than the Mohammedans.

The Hindu women are in the minority in proportion to the men, the ratio being eight to ten. This may be partly due to the mortality from smallpox being greater among female children, who are nursed less carefully. Children are married at an early age. Many girls become widows before they are ten years old and they are not allowed to re-marry. Young Hindu widows are exposed to special dangers to character and often lead unhappy lives. On the other hand, widowers may re-marry and often do so. Polygamy, although permitted, is rare—perhaps owing to the relatively small number of women.

The Hindu's whole life, from the hour of his birth till the day when he dies and his son sets light to his funeral pyre, is regulated by an elaborate code of religious rites, ceremonies and customs. These involve daily worship with ablutions and offerings to idols of flowers and food, frequent fastings, and the observance of a very large number of holy days.

As we continue to traverse the crowded streets, a line of laden ponies is driven with shouts and objurgations through the throng, or a solitary rider with many cries of "hosh hosh" makes his way along. But there is hardly any wheeled traffic.

Of the city population more than a half are provision sellers or artificers. This includes some 25,000 engaged in the wool industry. The most important trades are—grain dealers, vegetable and fruit sellers, dairymen, butchers, workers in metal and shoemakers. On either side of the road there is a deep gutter. Five feet above this are the open shop windows with stalls and shelves, one above another, laden with articles of commerce—piles of cotton

Photo by] [*R. E. Shorter*

14. SRINAGAR CITY. SHAH-I-HAMADÁN MOSQUE.

(Behind is the Hari Parbat hill and fort. The snowy peak is Kótwál.)

cloth, bottles of ghee, blocks of rock-salt, baskets of grain, maize, rice, lentils, flour, walnuts and sacks of turmeric. Here is a row of stalls with brass pots and pans and cooking-vessels; a little further on the deafening clang assails the ear of a copper-worker's shop, where large saucepans and boilers of all sorts are being hammered into shape. In other shops there are heaps of red earthenware pottery, rows of native shoes, saddlery, embroidery, large iron pans full of boiling syrup and piles of round slabs of sugar. Then we pass a line of bakers' shops with rows of wheaten and maize cakes and large flat chapattis like the unleavened bread of the Jews, and it is wonderful how like in appearance to Jews many of the people are. There is a curious legend, invented by the founder of the heretical Mohammedan Quadiani sect, to the effect that an ancient grave in Kashmir, of a saint named Yuz-ásaf, who died in the fifteenth century, is really the grave of Christ, who did not die on the cross, but escaped from the Holy Land to Kashmir. This legend is not, however, accepted by the Kashmiri Mussulmans.

As we walk through the city we pass several shrines of this kind with a surrounding enclosure and latticed windows. Right and left open filthy lanes and alleys, leading to court-yards and dark little staircases. Most of the houses are two-storied, but some are higher. The upper stories have latticed windows. In the winter paper is pasted over. There are comparatively few glass windows.

The population of a large and insanitary city like this, with the houses huddled together, suffers greatly from disease and poverty. The clan and family system, in some respects so admirable in the East, to a considerable extent obviates actual want except in times of great scarcity. But disease is rampant. The local hakíms, although some of them skilled in the empirical use of certain drugs and simples handed down by tradition, have no knowledge of anatomy or physiology. And in their use of drastic purgatives, venesection and absolute starvation, their practice approximates to that of the worst period of the Middle Ages in Europe. Those who succumb most readily are the young and the aged. I have frequently been called in to see patients quite healthy a few days before, but attacked by some comparatively simple ailment, who, by the reckless treatment of native practitioners, have been rapidly brought to death's door, and in many cases have actually died.

Of native surgery there is little in Kashmir. The barbers are fortunately not enterprising. When they do interfere, the chief effect is usually to produce unskilled wounds and inoculate them with the germs of putrefaction or even disease. The worst phase of both the medical and surgical indigenous practice is the fatal delay imposed, by which so many cases of curable disease drift into hopeless stages before they resort to better trained practitioners. Hardly a week passes without cases of this kind being brought to us.

The veil over the moral condition of such a city as Srinagar cannot be lifted. Suffice it to say that in many respects it is like that of Rome in its worst periods.

Among this mass of evil, misery and disease, quiet steady efforts have been put forth for some years by all too small a number of workers connected with the Church Missionary and Church of England Zenana Missionary Societies. The Rev. J. Hinton Knowles devoted the best years of his life to unremitting efforts on behalf of the Kashmir people. Miss Butler, a lady doctor, Miss Irene Petrie and Miss Robinson, a trained nurse, laid down their lives in Kashmir for the same cause. The late Revs. J. S. Doxey and C. E. Barton also rendered valuable service. For many years Miss E. G. Hull worked among the women, until, to our great regret and with serious loss to Kashmir, she was compelled by failing health to retire in 1909. Schools for girls have been carried on by Miss Churchill Taylor, Miss Stubbs and Miss Goodall. And for many years much nursing and medical relief have been given by Miss Newman. Since 1905 Miss Kate Knowles, M.B., London, has been ably carrying on and successfully developing medical work on behalf of the women of the city. Two other agencies, which for many years have been engaged in grappling with the moral and physical evils of Kashmir, are the Medical Mission and the Schools of the Church Missionary Society. The work of these may, however, be more fully considered in detail.

CHAPTER V

THE KASHMIR MISSION SCHOOL

In All Things be Men—An Original Method of Marking—Practical Philanthropy—The Goddess Káli and the Hooligans—A Crocodile Scare—Head of the River—An Unwilling Passenger—Visitation of Cholera—Knight-Errants—Education in India, its Needs and Defects.

> Make knowledge circle with the winds,
> But let her herald, reverence, fly
> Before her to whatever sky
> Bear seed of men and growth of minds!
>
> TENNYSON.

MANY of the chief objects of interest in Srinagar are suggestive of a certain greatness, glory and activity in the remote past. It is interesting to turn from these to a centre which is full of life at the present time and of hope for the future. More than fifty years ago, under circumstances of some difficulty, educational work was started by the late Dr Elmslie, the first medical missonary in Kashmir. But it was not until the time of the Rev. J. Hinton Knowles in 1884 that distinct progress was evident. The work thus fairly started was taken up by the Rev. C. E. Tyndale-Biscoe, who was joined in 1905 by an Oxford Honours man, the Rev. F. E. Lucey. The Mission School with its numerous branches is now a remarkable source of well-directed energy.

The central school is in a large house abutting on the river immediately above the third bridge. There is a fairly spacious playground attached, but the building is inadequate for the large number of scholars who attend. The work is carried on in an absolutely original manner. In the Srinagar Mission School there are altogether about 1500 scholars. The character of the Kashmiri boy is not good. He is often studious, but is usually untruthful, conceited, superstitious, cowardly, selfish and extremely dirty. The motto of this school is—" In all things be men." "The crest is a pair of paddles crossed. The paddles represent hard work or strength, the blade of the paddles being in the shape of a heart reminds them of kindness (the true man is a combination of strength and kindness). The crossed paddles represent self-sacrifice, reminding them from Whom we get the greatest example and from Whom we learn to be true men."

All over the city, boys may be met who wear this badge and they may be appealed to by any one in difficulty, distress or danger, as they have been taught to be ready to render service at all times to those who are in need.

The object of the principal of the school, the Rev. Cecil Tyndale-Biscoe, is to train *all* his boys and not only those who are clever or strong. In a little book entitled *Training in Kashmir*, he explains his methods. " We give fewer marks to mind than body because Kashmiri boys prefer their books to their bodily exercise. Marks in sports are not given necessarily to the best cricketer or swimmer but to the boy who tries most. If we always reward the strong, as is the custom of the world, we discourage the weak and often they give up trying. The energy of the staff is not concentrated on turning out a great cricket eleven, or great anything, for all those boys who are good at any particular sport are naturally keen and do not need spurring on; where the stress comes, is in the case of the weak, feeble, timid boys; it is they who require attention; it is they who specially need physical training and careful watching. Of course this system does not make a brave show, for the strength is given to the bulk and not to make brilliancy more brilliant. We are working for the future, the race of life, and must therefore fit all the boys for it, not a few special ones in order to make a show. Then again sports are not entered into for sport's sake, but for the results. Boys should have strong bodies so that they may help others who have weak ones. Again boys are not rewarded by prizes for sports, as we feel that true sport in the West is being killed by 'pot-hunting.' We pit one school against another, giving marks to the school and not to the boys, and the school that wins the greatest number of marks in regattas and sports wins the challenge cup. In this way we hope to take the selfishness out of games and create a true desire for honour for the school and community, as opposed to the individual."

The method of marking adopted in this school gives an idea of the thoroughness of the education, and will show the immense value of such an institution, both from a moral and political standpoint. One-third of the possible marks is allotted for moral proficiency, one-third for physical, and the remaining third for scholarship. The advantages of this are not only that every boy has a chance, but above all that the boys are trained to regard conduct and good citizenship as at least as important as book learning, and that sound bodies are as necessary as sound minds. With regard to conduct, it is not passive good behaviour that gains marks, but actual deeds of kindness. The activities of the Mission School are very varied. A large fire breaks out in the city and spreads with the utmost rapidity among the wooden houses, 3000 of which are burnt. The school work is stopped for the day and the principal and boys take along their fire-engine and fight the flames, sometimes at risk to their own lives, saving those of women and children in danger. The protection of women from insult, kindness to old people and invalids, the rescue of those in peril of drowning, and prevention of cruelty to animals, are some of the works of ministry, which the boys are encouraged to undertake. Although Brahmans may not touch a donkey, they may drive it or lead it with a rope. And one winter hospitality was shown by the Mission School to over a hundred starving donkeys, some of which would certainly have otherwise perished in the streets, where they are sent by their owners to pick up food as best they can.

Physical training includes gymnastics, drill, boating,

swimming, football and cricket, and the aim is to make the boys healthy and strong, promote *esprit de corps*, discipline, reverence for authority and a due sense of obedience and subordination. In scholarship there is an ordinary curriculum, including daily Bible lessons. Many of the boys are very young and their instruction elementary. Of the seniors not a few have successfully passed the matriculation examination of the Punjab University. In connection with the school there is a sanitary corps, which, armed with pick and shovel, will often give an object lesson to the people of Srinagar by visiting some specially dirty court or lane and showing the inhabitants what is required to keep it clean. Sometimes, too, at the hospital a group of Mission School boys arrives to take out convalescents for an airing on the lake, where they provide tea at their own expense and bring them safely back in the evening.

A site for a dispensary is granted by H.H. the Maharajah to Miss Newman, who is doing such good work among the women of Kashmir. The site is on top of a hill, and quarter of a mile away down below, a great heap of stones is dumped by the side of the lake. The principal proposes that the schoolboys should make these stones walk up-hill. So one evening nearly four hundred of the boys, with many masters, line out from the lake to the hill-top and hand on the stones just like, at city fires, they have often passed on buckets. That Brahman teachers and boys should do hard work of this kind provoked much opposition. Some jeered, others indulged in chaff, and a few cursed the willing labourers and said they were bringing dishonour on their caste. But the idea took root; old boys of the school came and joined in, and on the second day there were other recruits, and the opposition died away.

In Eastern cities there are often bands of hooligans who terrorize the people, insult women and molest small boys. The police are often for various reasons unable or unwilling to deal with these pestilent gangs. With the help of the school organization, some of these rascals have been from time to time brought to justice. The following is a characteristic incident. "Some Punjabis, probably soldiers, had come to a fair for no good intention, and soon were at their game, molesting some Hindu women, who had come to worship; but no one in the crowd came forward to protect these women. Fortunately, however, some Mission School boys arrived on the scene, and they at once fell upon these hooligans and smote them hip and thigh. And when the crowd perceived which way the battle was going, it joined very wisely the winning side. As this little affair happened at the shrine of the goddess of murder, I asked the staff and boys which side the goddess took in the fight? This question was rather a poser, for some said that the goddess was on the side of those who attacked the women, and others maintained that she sided with the schoolboys. Opinions were divided on this important subject until a Solomon solved the difficulty by explaining that as Káli was the goddess of murder and blood, she would naturally side with the party which shed the most blood, and that honour certainly fell to the Mission School boys. This decision pleased and comforted us all."

In the summer every boy has to bathe daily with his class. Those who cannot swim are placed under the care of swimmers until they themselves learn. Sometimes there are as many as 300 boys in the water at once. At the end of the term there is usually a long swim. About seventy boys take part in this. They are accompanied by a fleet of boats, in case there should be need of rescuing. The ordinary long-distance swim is three or four miles across the Dal Lake. Some of the boys become such strong swimmers that they can do eight or nine miles. One of the practical results of this swimming is the saving of life. In one year alone eight lives were saved, and in two cases at great risk to the rescuer. A medal is awarded in the school for especially meritorious cases of this kind (Plate 15).

15. SCHOOL SPORTS. A SPLASH DASH.

The following account, taken from a local paper, gives an illustration of the way in which the school influence is brought to bear on superstition:—

"Any one who visits the city of Srinagar in Kashmir in the summer-time and travels down the river between 6 and 8 a.m. will see hundreds of the Hindu inhabitants disporting themselves in the river, the older ones standing or squatting in shallow water at the ghats, combining their washing and devotions, and the younger ones enjoying short swims. But one day in July this pleasant state of things ended, for it was reported that a crocodile had visited Srinagar and had taken a fancy for bathers; so from that day till the end of August swimming and the like was stopped. Every one said they knew of people having been bitten, and many had seen the monster, which, of course, grew more terrible as time went on.

"When the Mission School boys reassembled after the summer vacation they took the matter in hand. A hundred of them started to swim the whole length of the city from the first to the seventh bridge, a distance of 3 miles, and defy the monster. Their daring was watched by thousands of inhabitants from the banks, bridges and houses, making a brave show. Thirty-three swimmers reached the last bridge and others found the water too cold and left the water at the school half-way. The result of the swim has been that the inhabitants have come to the conclusion that the crocodile has left Srinagar, and they are now enjoying their morning bathe once more."

The principal of the school, who was "Cox" to a winning Cambridge boating crew in 1885, has kept up his aquatic interests, and every year the crew of the branch and central Mission Schools have a keen competition for "head of the river."

All this work has not been achieved without an up-hill struggle. At one time the State authorities tried to put a stop to it. But the greatest of all difficulties was the influence of caste and the temperament of the Kashmiri. To play with cricket or footballs, which are covered with leather, and to paddle or row a boat were considered absolutely against caste principles. To go out after dark was considered risky because evil spirits are supposed to patrol the streets at that time. The boys were naturally studious but disinclined for athletics, and they were much given to tale-telling. The prime object of education was supposed to be to fit them to earn money for themselves and their families; for early marriage is the custom of the East, and many boys are already married. The great task to which Mr Tyndale-Biscoe addressed himself, was to teach the boys manliness, loyalty, charity, manners, cleanliness, truth and Christian doctrine. Speaking of those early days the principal of the school says: "I knew it would be a long fight but had no idea it would be such a hard one. Now it was not until the sixth year of our commencing backbone and knuckle work that the first Kashmiri boat propelled by Kashmiri paddles in the hands of fifteen Brahmans splashed down the Jhelum, not in a secluded quiet spot in the lake, but right down the city of Srinagar itself, under bridges crowded with jeering townsmen; however, in order that they might not altogether and entirely dishonour their own families, each boy covered his head with a blanket, with the exception of the steersman, so that their individual identity might not be known.

"This crew came not from the High School. The honour of being the first school to brave public opinion fell to the Renawári Branch School, under the plucky leadership of Amar Chand Brahman, who has since those days shown much pluck and grit; but perhaps this first effort to break away from the shackles of idiotic custom, cost him most of all. Now that the ball had been set rolling, or rather that the first crew had been set paddling, it was not long before other school Kashmiri boats called 'shikáras' were launched, until a fleet gradually came into existence, which now numbers ten boats, holding roughly 120 boys. The Rena-

16. FLEET PADDLING PAST THE HIGH SCHOOL.

wári School crew in the yearly race for headship of the river held the position for six years in succession."

In 1891, when Lord Lansdowne, who was then Viceroy of India, was in Kashmir, he witnessed one of these exciting contests, and expressed a hope that the State and Mission Schools would ere long be competing in friendly contest for the headship of the Jhelum, as Oxford and Cambridge Universities strive yearly for the headship of the Thames. Eighteen years passed, and at last the Viceroy's hope was fulfilled. On 20th September 1909, a race took place between the Mission, State, Hindoo and Islamic schools over a two-mile course. The Mission School crew won by thirty lengths. It is hoped that this will prove the first of a long series of annual races, in which case it must be regarded as an historic and interesting sign of the development of physical culture in Kashmir (Plate 16).

These aquatic sports are not without their amusing incidents. " It was the summer of a great cholera epidemic, and the citizens were by no means in a jovial frame of mind; in fact their minds dwelt chiefly on the three stages of cholera and burning ghats. We thought a change of ideas might be good for them, so we brought our fleet from the lake to the city, and had boat races in the afternoons, over which we made a good deal of noise, so that both boys and onlookers forgot about corpses and pyres, and enjoyed an hour or so of fun and laughter instead. These races incidentally proved that we did not take a gloomy view of things in general or of cholera in particular. Now, as several were racing down-stream abreast, in their excitement the boys had not noticed an omnibus or passenger boat coming upstream, and before they were aware of this danger, one of the boats was steered straight into the omnibus, picked off an old woman who was sitting in the boat and carried her off down-stream, like a figure-head, at the end of the prow. Our hearts were in our mouths in a moment and a dead silence followed, for all feared that the old lady had become a fixture to the prow of the boat, as the Kashmir boats have a very sharp nose tipped with iron. In a few moments, however, the racing boat was stopped with the aid of fifteen paddles hard astern, and the old lady was once more deposited in her former boat in a moister condition than when she left it; and almost before we had time to ask questions, the dear dishevelled, dripping old lady clenched her fist and gave tongue at the boys in her Kashmiri best, which would have put even Billingsgate hawkers to shame. Our pent-up feelings simply went flop. We all to a man rose to our feet and gave the loud-lunged lady three ringing cheers, and the louder we cheered the more she cursed, until distance prevented our hearing the remainder of her vocabulary. We have never carried off a damsel from a passing boat since that day, as our coxens have learnt that when they wish to have ladies aboard, it is wiser to 'easy' first, then hand them in without unseemly haste."

Some years ago a fleet of four boats started down the river to the Wular Lake. They had very dirty weather from start to finish. Crossing the lake, a mast was smashed and the mainsail blown away. Later on the breeze worked up into a gale. It was necessary to cross 7 miles of lake to reach their camp. The boatmen on the shore implored them not to go, saying that it was impossible to cross in such weather. After a very rough time, in which the boys showed much pluck, they reached their camp in the dark. Next morning one of their broken oars was washed ashore at Bandipoora, and a clerk telegraphed up to the city that all the crew must have perished. This caused quite a sensation in Srinagar. When, some days later, the fleet returned, the bridges and banks were crowded with spectators, who cheered the boys as they rowed past.

Srinagar is liable to constantly recurring floods. These usually occur in the summer, if there is continuous rain, when the snow is still abundant on the mountains around. When the river is very high, if an embankment should burst or be topped, a district which was dry in the morning may a few hours later be a lake, with the houses, which are built of sun-dried bricks, falling down in all directions. On one occasion over 2000 houses fell in or around the city. On these occasions the Mission School boats are able to do yeoman service, rescuing families which are stranded on the roofs of rickety houses or small patches of dry ground.

That a Mark Tapley-like spirit is inculcated in the Mission School would appear from the following incident.

"There is fortunately a bright side to everything in this life, even if it is the darkest of clouds; and cholera is no exception to the rule. We cheer ourselves and the boys with the thought that there will be many opportunities for playing the man, and what more inspiring incentive can one have than this?

"On one occasion some time ago, when we had a very severe epidemic of cholera, we put this side of the picture so forcibly before the boys, that the whole school stood up and gave three hearty cheers for the cholera. I am afraid that a certain number of those who cheered were never given another opportunity of cheering a second visitation, for the school gave its quota to that fell disease, though the staff tried hard to save their boys, adding nursing to their other duties. One of the masters was attacked, and when, late one evening, on his rounds, Mr Tyndale-Biscoe visited him, he found some of the other masters, with their coats off, doing their best by massage to relieve the terrible pain of cramp from which he was suffering, and they had arranged to take turns, two hours at a time, in watching him all night. Mr Tyndale-Biscoe says: "I had just given him a teaspoonful of brandy, when the man who was holding his head said to me in a whisper, 'Please, Sahib, leave the room.' Thinking that it was on account of Hindu women present, I did so. Early next morning the man came to tell me that the teacher was dead. I asked the time of his death; he answered: 'Directly you put the brandy in his mouth, but

I did not tell any one of the relations for fear that they would say that you had killed him; also on account of the women, for women bear bad news better in the morning than at night, and we massaged his limbs so that those in the room might not know that he was dead till the sun arose.'

"There were these teachers massaging a cholera corpse all night, and they knew well the risk they ran of infection, but they stuck to it in order to save me and lessen the shock for the women relations."

Various societies are worked by the masters and boys. For the former, there is a Provident Fund to which all have to pay five per cent. of their salaries and the object of which is to make provision for old age and sickness and provide for their widows should they die. Another useful organization is the "waif and stray" society, to which all masters and boys subscribe and thereby pay for the schooling of fifty poor boys, and feed and clothe those who need it. At a recent meeting in connection with this society the case was reported of a master who had recently died of consumption, leaving his family very badly off. The principal asked those present what they proposed doing. The secretary stood up and said: "We must support this family ourselves. I myself will be responsible for so much, and I am sure all you present" (looking round upon his brother masters) "will do the same." The motion was carried *nem. con.*

The Knight-Errant Society has as its object the raising of the status of women in Kashmir. Many of the young Hindus are now really anxious to abolish evil customs. The Knights pledge themselves to do all in their power to prevent girls being married under the age of fourteen.

It is often extremely difficult to ascertain the truth in the case of criminal charges and counter-charges which are so common in the East. To assist in such matters, a court-martial has been constituted in the Mission School, which not only deals with cases of this kind brought by or against masters and boys, but it also takes cognizance of offences committed by former scholars who have misbehaved in the public offices or the city.

Throughout the whole of the remarkable organization of this unique school, the guiding principle is to *lead the way*, to show the masters and boys that the great aim of Christianity and the great call of the Christian Church is to Service. Scripture teaching is given day by day in the classes, but this is only the beginning of the education. The next and by far the more important part is to *put the teaching into practice.*

Mr Tyndale-Biscoe is no doubt fortunate in the scope which he has in Kashmir for carrying out education on such original lines. And the praiseworthy tolerance of the Kashmir State authorities is a remarkable sign of enlightenment. The Maharajah of Kashmir has subscribed to the schools and often spoken words of cheer to the boys, and recently His Highness granted an excellent site for a Hostel. Although there must be much in the school methods which must be trying and even irritating to old-fashioned and orthodox Hindus, still the influence for good has been so obvious that it has been accepted with gratitude by the Hindu authorities of the Kashmir State and recognized to be of the utmost value to the moral evolution of Kashmir.

Mr Tyndale-Biscoe's school is of course unique, and his methods most original; but it is cheering to remember that hundreds of mission schools and colleges throughout India are carrying on work in the same spirit of practical Christianity, and training boys and young men to be good and loyal citizens and mindful of the needs of others. It is amazing to find what a very large number of Indian gentlemen, occupying positions of authority and influence, received their education in mission schools.

As the boys pass out of the schools and occupy various posts of importance, it is easy to see that this work has a very wide reach. Only those who have studied the subject realize the extent to which, throughout India, mission schools have trained those who are now wielding power both in Native States like Kashmir and in the British Provinces. Unfortunately Mohammedans have been less influenced by education than the Hindus. The Islamic brotherhood is very conservative in matters of education, and in Kashmir it forms more than ninety per cent. of the population.

Of the awakening of India there are now many signs. Especially during the last quarter of a century have the solvent influences of the West been obviously permeating the whole fabric of Indian society; and now in India we have a changed outlook and a unique condition of affairs. Various nations, whose chief bonds of union are religious, and whose own systems are extremely rigid and intensely conservative and unprogressive, and who, in the Native States, are accustomed to a rule far more despotic than that of the British Government, are now beginning to show signs of fermentation. The new wine of the West has been poured into old bottles, and the bottles are in danger of bursting. New political ideas have infiltrated the educated classes, and visions of Home Rule to be obtained by political agitation, in which boycott and bombs are also to be weapons, are leading to what may be a great upheaval.

The greatest factor in bringing about this portentous change has been education. Throughout the length and breadth of the land, schools and colleges have been at work. The Government of India has had magnificent opportunities for educating the people of India. The seed which it has sown has produced the harvest which is now ripening—a mixed harvest of good and bad. Most excellent work has been done. Schools and colleges and institutions for technical training have been multiplied throughout the land. In the universities a high standard has been aimed at, and in some of the faculties the examinations are said to be actually more difficult than those in the corresponding subjects in British Universities. And yet the education has admittedly been a failure in one direction, and that the most important of all. It has been purely secular and far too Western. Indian students have been set to study Stuart Mill, Herbert Spencer and Huxley. But

> "Knowledge is a barren tree and bare,
> Bereft of God."

A structure of modern political economy and science has been reared upon a foundation which is unsound and cannot bear the strain. Moral instruction has, until quite recently, been absolutely ignored. In accordance with its principles of religious neutrality, the Indian Government has been unable to give any religious training in Government schools; and so the greatest motive for upright conduct, the belief in a living and righteous God, has been withheld, and from our Government schools and colleges have come, in their tens of thousands, boys and young men, clever and well-educated on the intellectual side, but with the moral side undeveloped—young men, Western to a considerable extent in intellectual attainment and political aim, and Eastern in moral character and home life. But are not the Eastern people very religious? Yes, but the word religious has a different significance in the East and West. In the East a man may be regarded as most religious and holy whose life is untrue and unclean. Indeed such a man may even be the revered religious teacher of thousands, who in no way regard his impure life as any barrier to sanctity.

The extent to which missionary enterprise has stepped in to save the situation is not realized in the United Kingdom. But still, compared with the immense population, far too little has been done, and Government schools are in the great majority. At first the Missionary Societies looked askance at the development of educational work, which they regarded as secular and unproductive of converts. Gradually a change has occurred, and we now find most of them actively engaged in this work. Their efforts, too, have been appreciated even by orthodox Hindus, who openly say that they prefer Mission Schools because of the moral training given. Most of the large towns of India have important Mission Schools or Colleges, as, for instance, the educational work of the Church Missionary Society in Bombay, Calcutta, Agra, Allahabad and Peshawar, and the splendid work of the Cambridge Mission at Delhi, of the S.P.G. at Cawnpore, of the Oxford Mission at Calcutta and of American Missionary Societies in Lahore and Bombay. The Scottish Presbyterian Missions have also done yeoman service in education in India, and the names of Dr Duff and Dr Miller are well known.

Dr Duff predicted nearly three-quarters of a century ago, with remarkable accuracy, the present state of affairs. He said:

"If in that land you do give the people knowledge without religion, rest assured that it is the greatest blunder, politically speaking, that ever was committed. Having free unrestricted access to the whole range of our English-speaking literature and science, they will despise and reject their own absurd system of learning. Once driven out of their own systems, they will inevitably become infidels in religion. And shaken out of the mechanical round of their own religious observances, without moral principles to balance their thoughts or guide their movements, they will as certainly become discontented, restless agitators, ambitious of power and official distinction and possessed of the most disloyal sentiments towards that Government which, in their eye, has usurped all the authority that rightly belonged to themselves. This is not theory, it is fact."

A scheme has been recently put forward, which, if it could be put into general practice, would do much to remove the reproach at present resting upon the Government of India. The ideal scheme for giving religious and moral training without compromising the neutrality of Government is that residential colleges should be established. The boys are to live in hostels, each of which will be a private institution and have its own religious instruction. Some of the hostels will be Christian, some Mohammedan, and some Hindu. The college itself will be a Government Institution and in it religion will not be taught. Whether this or some similar scheme is introduced, there is a widespread feeling, that so far education in India has been conspicuously defective on the moral side. This was emphasized in the answers returned by several Indian Ruling Chiefs to a communication addressed to them by the Viceroy on the subject of the prevailing unrest in India. The Maharajah of Kashmir expressed a strong opinion as to the importance of proper education not only for boys but for girls too.

In this work, both in the Plains of India and in Kashmir, Mission Schools have been pioneers.

CHAPTER VI

THE KASHMIR MEDICAL MISSION

Early Days—Robert Clark—A Threatening Mob—The First Convert—Dr Elmslie—Opposition—Development and Progress—Famine Relief—The Great Earthquake—Fighting Cholera, Smallpox and Plague.

> There lies no desert in the land of life;
> For e'en that tract that barrenest doth seem,
> Laboured of thee in faith and hope shall teem
> With heavenly harvests and rich gatherings rife.
>
> FRANCES KEMBLE.

THE founder of the Kashmir Mission was the Rev. Robert Clark. In 1854 Colonel Martin, an officer who had just retired from his command at Peshawar, proposed to Mr Clark a missionary tour in Kashmir, Ladákh and Skardo. They were accompanied by three Indian Christians. Gulab Singh, the Maharajah of Kashmir, accorded them a friendly reception. But he was rather cynical. "My subjects in Kashmir," he said, "are very bad. I am sure that no one can do them any harm. I am rather curious to see whether the padri sahibs can do them any good."

On his return from this tour Mr Clark powerfully represented the needs of Kashmir. He received much support from a group of leading civilians and military men, including Sir Robert Montgomery, then Lieutenant-Governor of the Punjab. "A requisition, influentially supported, was immediately sent to the Church Missionary Society, urging it to promote a Mission in the mountain kingdom, and the Lieutenant-Governor was the first to sign the invitation. His donation of a thousand rupees, in aid of the proposed Mission, was the nucleus of a fund that the generous liberality of friends rapidly augmented to over fourteen thousand rupees."[1] This invitation was accepted by the C.M.S., and Mr Smith of Benares was appointed and joined Mr Clark in Kashmir in 1863; but it was not until the following year that the work was fairly started.

The first attempt to carry on systematic Medical Mission work in Kashmir met with much opposition. Some of the officials, especially the governor and the head of the police, were most antagonistic, and permitted, if they did not actually organize, mob violence. The Rev. R. Clark made the following entry in his diary written in 1864: "The house was literally besieged with men and noisy boys. They stood by hundreds on the bridge, and lined the river on both sides, shouting, and one man striking a gong, to collect the people. Not a chuprasse, or police officer, or soldier, or official of any kind appeared. The tumult quickly increased, and no efforts were made to stop it. The people began to throw stones and some of them broke down the wall of the compound and stables. Our servants became greatly alarmed, for they threatened to burn the house down. The number present was between one thousand and one thousand five hundred. When I went to the Wazir to ask for protection, it was said that he was asleep. He kept me waiting for two hours and then did not even give me a chair. He promised to send a guard and never did so. The police also announced that if any one rented a house to the missionaries, all the skin would be taken off their backs."

On 20th April Mr Clark writes in his journal: "Men are again stationed on the bridge, as they were for weeks together last year, to prevent any one from coming to us. Our servants cannot buy the mere necessaries of life and we have to send strangers to the other end of the city to purchase flour."

The house which Mr and Mrs Clark occupied was near the sixth bridge. Mrs Clark started a dispensary for women

[1] Martyn Clark, *Robert Clark of the Punjab.*

almost in the exact place where the Diamond Jubilee Hospital, so ably conducted by Miss Lauder, is now situated. Sometimes in one day as many as one hundred women came to Mrs Clark for medical treatment.

Official antagonism, however, continued. The names of those who visited Mr Clark were reported. A Punjabi officer in the State artillery was told that unless he removed his two boys from instruction by Mr Clark he would be cashiered "and made to beg his bread from door to door."

Of Husn Shah, the first Kashmiri convert to be baptized, Mr Clark writes: "He has been with us now nearly a year, has been imprisoned continually, and had logs of wood tied to his feet; has been beaten, threatened and promised all sorts of things by the Wazir himself, if he would leave us. Never has he been left in peace. Day after day has he been tried and tempted by mother and friends, and coaxed and punished by those in authority, but apparently in vain; for he has hitherto resisted or endured all." A trumped-up charge of debt was brought against him. First twenty-five rupees was claimed, then fifty. When security was offered for this amount the claim was suddenly raised to seven hundred rupees.

Opposition continued till the end of the season, when Mr Clark left Srinagar for the Punjab on 2nd November. Almost the last thing he witnessed as he was dropping down the river in a house-boat, was the arrest of a young man, who had been under Christian instruction. "He was carried away," Mr Clark writes, "before my very face to answer before the Wazir, and to suffer imprisonment, for wishing to be a Christian and visiting the missionary. No other crime was ever spoken of."

Dr Elmslie, who was the first Medical Missionary appointed by the C.M.S., arrived in Kashmir the following year, 1865. At that time no European was allowed to remain in the valley for the winter. During the summer, about 2000 patients came to Dr Elmslie. But his experiences were similar to those of Mr Clark. And when he left Kashmir at the close of the season, the Governor of Kashmir told the owner of the house which Dr Elmslie had occupied, that he was on no account to let it again to the doctor the following year.

In 1866, unable to obtain adequate accommodation, Dr Elmslie pitched the outer covering of a large tent for the use of his out-patients, and the inner part of the same tent was all the accommodation for in-patients which he could provide. During that season he had, however, 3365 patients.

For three years Dr Elmslie revisited the valley of Kashmir each summer, and by his kindness and skill continued to gain the confidence of the people, in spite of the opposition of the local authorities, and the fact that the avenues leading to his house were closely watched by sepoys, who intimidated the sick people and exacted money from them.

A widespread cholera epidemic in 1867, while diminishing the number of ordinary patients, gave the Medical Mission the opportunity of helping the cholera-stricken.

When Dr Elmslie laid down his work in 1869, he had achieved much. The opposition of the State authorities had been, to a considerable extent, overcome; the confidence of the Kashmiris had been won, and an immense amount of relief had been afforded to sufferers. Four Kashmiris had become Christians. One of these for many years continued to render faithful service in Kashmir as a Christian teacher. As an indirect result of the work of the Medical Mission, the first Kashmir State Dispensary had been started. And this was the forerunner of the present extensive State Medical Service.

In 1870 the Rev. W. T. Storrs, a qualified medical man, carried on the work during Dr Elmslie's absence on furlough. In 1872 Dr Elmslie returned and worked with untiring assiduity at Srinagar, where cholera was again raging. His death took place in the autumn of that year at Gujrat, on his way from Kashmir to the Punjab.

Dr Theodore Maxwell, who was Elmslie's successor, was fortunate in meeting with a very friendly reception from the Maharajah Ranbir Singh, who, hearing that Maxwell was a nephew of General John Nicholson of Delhi fame, promised to grant good house accommodation.

The work was reopened in 1874 under favourable conditions. Official opposition was withdrawn. The State medical officer was friendly. The Maharajah granted a site for a hospital, and at State expense a small building was erected on the north side of the Rustum Gaddi Hill.

After two years of most successful work, Dr Maxwell's health broke down, and he was compelled to leave India.

A well-known Indian Christian doctor, John Williams, for many years most honourably associated with the little frontier town of Tank, came to the rescue, and with the help of the Rev. T. R. Wade, whose valued services to the Kashmir Medical Mission can hardly be over-estimated, he carried on the work so vigorously that there was no falling off in the number of patients.

In 1877 Dr Edmund Downes, who had resigned a commission in the Royal Artillery in order to engage in Medical Mission work, arrived in Kashmir. For six years he carried on the work steadily and bravely in spite of ill-health and inadequate assistance. Owing to his skill and surgical enterprise, the reputation of the hospital continued to rise and the number of patients consequently to increase. From 1877-1879 Kashmir was visited by an appalling famine. In some parts of the valley, including Srinagar, it is said that the population was reduced by more than a half. Heavy rain fell in the autumn, before the crops were gathered in. The rice and maize which are the staple foods rotted. During the winter, rain continued. The cattle died from want of food. The spring harvest failed owing to bad weather. The authorities made a fatal mistake and ordered a house-to-house search for seed-grain, which the cultivators had stored for spring use. Believing, probably with good reason, that this grain would be confiscated by tyrannous and absolutely unprincipled officials, the people consumed the seed-grain themselves, or by hiding it in damp places they so damaged it that it was no longer available for sowing. As a result, the famine continued until October 1879. Oil-cake, rice, chaff, the bark of the elm and yew, and even grasses and roots were eagerly devoured by the starving people, who became absolutely demoralized and like ravenous beasts, each struggling for his own life. The corpses of those who had perished were left lying or hastily dragged to the nearest well or hole, until these became choked with dead bodies. Dogs wandered about in troops preying upon the unburied carcases. Pestilence dogged the steps of want and cholera broke out. Everything combined to intensify the disaster. Many officials in high places proved apathetic, or worse still, for selfish purposes, aided and abetted in keeping up prices, and even intercepting the grain which was being sent in over rough mountain tracks for the relief of the dying.

Speaking of 1878, Mr Wade says: " To-day I have ridden through a great part of the city, and I saw a large number of persons, especially children and women, whom death certainly has marked for his own very shortly. A half-dozen times I tried to buy and distribute some kulchas—small cakes made of the flour of Indian corn, rice or wheat—and was as often mobbed. Poor children crept from underneath the verandah boards of closed shops, and others from holes and corners that pariah dogs generally occupy, and surrounded my pony. Parda women, and apparently most respectable men, stopped and begged and struggled for a piece of bread. I found it impossible to keep the people from thronging me, or to maintain anything like order. Directly I obtained any kulchas, the hungry pressed upon me, the stronger pushing aside the weaker, and all reaching forth their hands, and begging or screaming, they laid hold of my coat. They took bread out of my pockets. Two men with baskets of bread, from whom I attempted to purchase some, were besieged and their bread speedily seized and eaten. After having paid for the bread, I made my escape by riding as fast as I could away from the hungry crowd."

Mr Wade did splendid work in this famine. He employed a very large number of coolies on famine relief works, and made and repaired roads, dug and cleaned canals, filled up foul holes, levelled uneven ground and planted trees. Many of the most familiar land-marks, such as the lines of poplar trees, roads and canals in and around the Munshi Bagh, the European quarter of Srinagar, date back to this time. With foresight and faith in the future of the Medical Mission, Mr Wade had a great terrace cut across the north side of the Rustum Gaddi Hill, stretching eastwards from the clump of buildings already planted there by Dr Maxwell. This subsequently formed a magnificent site for the extension of the rapidly-growing and developing Mission Hospital (Plate 17).

Gratuitous relief was given regularly at the hospital. Sometimes as many as 2000 applicants assembled at one time. An orphanage was started with the help of Mrs Downes, and at one time there were as many as 400 inmates. When the famine had subsided, however, all the orphans were claimed by their friends.

Meanwhile the medical and surgical work of the Mission were steadily increasing. Dr Downes' reputation was attracting large numbers; and in 1878 as many as 1000 in-patients were treated in the hospital. Dr Downes also initiated district work, and made tours in the valley during which he saw over a thousand patients.

Thus Elmslie planted the Medical Mission, Maxwell found it a permanent home, and Downes consolidated and extended it, and especially built up a great surgical reputation. With the kind aid of the Kashmir State he enlarged the hospital, until there was accommodation for a hundred patients.

During three of the most disastrous years ever experi-

Photo by] [*G. W. Tyndale-Biscoe,*

17. THE KASHMIR MISSION HOSPITAL.

enced by Kashmir, when famine and disease were stalking like spectres through the land, Dr Downes and Mr Wade were thus unceasingly engaged, the one in combating disease, the other in fighting famine.

When in 1882 Dr Downes was compelled by ill-health to retire, a public farewell meeting was held. It was presided over by the British political officer on special duty, and addresses and testimonials were presented to him by patients and friends of various ranks, creeds and nationalities, testifying to the high esteem in which he was held by all who had come into contact with him.

Dr Arthur Neve arrived in Kashmir in March 1882. He enjoyed the great advantage of working with Dr Downes till the autumn, when he took over charge. Nineteen years later the Kaisar-i-Hind gold medal was conferred on him for Public Service. One of the greatest drawbacks to the satisfactory development of the Mission Hospital has always been the want of Indian Christian helpers. A hospital worked entirely with the aid of Hindu and Mohammedan subordinates is liable to the introduction of bribery and corruption, and not only do the patients suffer from neglect but even graver scandals may arise. Dr A. Neve brought with him from the Punjab two Indian Christians to fill the posts respectively of house-surgeon and chief dispenser. This marked a distinct advance. Both did excellent work. The house-surgeon, Hospital Assistant K. B. Thomas, after many years of faithful service, laid down his life in the terrible cholera epidemic of 1892, in which he had rendered most valuable aid.

Kashmir is a land of catastrophes, and in 1885 the great earthquake occurred. This is vividly described in a letter written by the Rev. Rowland Bateman at the time. " We went to a village 16 miles from Srinagar, itinerating, on 29th May. Before going to bed we heard a booming sound less unlike the report of distant ordnance than anything else, only it was evidently not distant at all. Being tired, we idly wondered what it was and forgot it. About three o'clock next morning there was a terrible shaking. Our village beds, at all time lively from other causes, began to dance about the room with us on them. The hut we were in was made of wood, and did not fall as the plaster did, so we were only smothered in dust. A large silk factory next door fell with a terrible crash. A piteous wail arose from all the inhabitants. Next morning we were in doubt which way to go, not knowing whether a similar shock had been felt in Srinagar. We decided to return. Not far from our door we saw the sole survivor of a family digging graves for his wife and child, his sister and her child. There were none wounded. Those who did not escape were dead. We trudged back through mud and rain to the city. The convulsion had been less and less severe in every village we reached, but just as we entered Srinagar we saw in one place twenty-one fires consuming the bodies of as many soldiers who were being summoned to parade as we passed the day before. The Mission Hospital was almost uninjured, though there was a sad loss in glass and drugs. We rested, I am sorry to say, on Sunday instead of going out as we should have done had we known that the district which we had been going to had suffered much more than the capital.

"On Monday Mr Knowles and I went out to collect the wounded in boats and bring them to the hospital which Dr Neve established on the river bank at Baramula. This work lasted for a fortnight. It was soon apparent that we had to count the dead by thousands. There can hardly have been less than three thousand deaths in the district we traversed in that time. The proportion of wounded to dead was everywhere surprisingly small, but there was plenty to do. And every day the cases became worse from neglect and delay. Bones began to reunite all crooked, dislocations to get hopelessly stiff, wounds to gangrene and mortify, and systems grew less able to bear the operations which earlier might have been unnecessary.

"The Kashmiris have a habit of taking little pitchers of live embers (kangris) with them to bed. These, of course, were broken, and the horrors of fire were added to those of mutilation. In some cases, where the houses were thatched, the roofs caught fire, and many were thus burned to death. Some classes of the people live under huge flat roofs covered with as much as 2 feet of earth. In these are collected all the live stock. One such I saw; it was about 60 feet by 25 feet. It had fallen so flat that you would not have recognized it as the site of a house at all. Under it were sleeping about one hundred head of cattle and sheep, and seventeen human beings. When I got there, three men, the sole survivors, were digging through the roof for fourteen corpses. They had pulled out a pony alive, but it died before it could get off the roof. Close by was a house where the diggers were rewarded by a child with half his scalp torn off, a boy with both feet shattered, and a man hopelessly crushed by a beam. Again, close by, was a woman with an infant at her breast and her arm badly broken. Her husband had escaped, but the sensitive fellow had fled from the horrors that surrounded him. I tried to persuade her to come with me, but she could not walk. All the beds had been smashed, so there was nothing to carry her upon. All the horses had been killed, so she could not ride; and at last when I proposed to see her safe to the hospital on a cow that was standing near, she said, 'Alas, sir, that cow has a broken leg.' We were put to strange shifts sometimes for ambulance. In some villages they could not get out the dead, in others there was not strength to bury them. Everywhere the stench was intolerable.

"I used to try and estimate the casualties by counting the new graves and fresh ash-heaps. But this expedient failed me in one hamlet at least, where out of forty-seven inhabitants only seven had escaped at all. Four of these were wounded and only two able-bodied men. How could they bury their dead? Nature provided an answer; and all along in the fresh clefts in the earth her victims were reverently laid. The convulsion that had destroyed them provided them with decent burial, and far below the level of the soil, green sods were laid on the deep graves of that awful graveyard.

"The people, though called Mohammedan, are much more like Hindus in their faith. Instead of devils or local gods they pray to 'pirs' or saints. In a village where a very celebrated tomb stands, the house, being wooden, had escaped. The people told me that the pir had saved them. We asked why the pir of a neighbouring village had not saved the people who lived round his tomb, and told them that we had seen the tomb itself upset, and the trees which overshadowed it torn 20 yards from one another. 'Oh,' they said, 'save them! Why should he? They had heaped too much earth upon him, the fools, and it was his turning in his grave to shake it off that caused their destruction.'

"It is something to have turned the thoughts of many of these people to the living God. The friendliness and sympathy we have shown them will make the missionary welcome when he returns to expound the way of God more perfectly. Some of those who owe their limbs or their lives to Christian medical effort will surely learn to love Him whose steps we were trying to follow, and so their calamity will be changed into a blessing.

"The destruction wrought by the earthquake has been fearful. Its exact extent may never be accurately known. But it is estimated that over 3000 persons have perished, that 10,000 houses have been wrecked, and 40,000 more cattle and sheep been destroyed. Many villages have been obliterated, and the towns of Sopur and Baramula exist, but as heaps of ruins."

In the early autumn the Maharajah Ranbir Singh died. Although at first opposed to the work of the Medical Mission, he had become distinctly friendly and helpful, and had not only granted a site but erected hospital buildings at State expense. He was a kingly man and a capable ruler.

Two decades had elapsed since Elmslie laid the foundation of the Medical Mission work. It is interesting to note the degree of progress. A large hospital, roughly constructed but capable of holding a hundred patients, was now the centre of a definite missionary organization, which had borne fruit in a small community of native Christians, and the New Testament had been translated by the Rev. T. R. Wade into Kashmiri.

In the winter of 1886 the hospital staff was augmented by the arrival of the writer. This doubling of the staff marked a notable advance, increasing as it did our capacity for work and our reach. For it now became possible to visit systematically outlying portions of Kashmir. Indeed in 1887 more patients were seen in the villages than at the central hospital.

Srinagar has been designated the City of the Sun. It might with equal propriety be called the City of Appalling Odours. The long streets by which it is traversed have been metalled and drained and made presentable, but countless lanes and alleys intersect the whole town. The population is extraordinarily dense. The people know nothing of sanitation and are primitive in their habits. Large areas of courtyard and lane are never penetrated by the rays of the sun. In wet weather the boots of the pedestrians sink deeply into evil-smelling black slime, which is being added to daily. In the summer, when the shade temperature is often over 90° F., it is dreadful to contemplate the variety of germs of disease and pestilence which may be multiplying in those foul recesses, as they seethe with the malodorous emanations from accumulated filth. The drainage runs into stagnant canals in which the people bathe and wash their clothes, and from which the women fill their water-pots with water for drinking and household use. In 1888 there was no supply of pure drinking-water laid on in the city. Srinagar, from a sanitary standpoint, was like a powder magazine waiting for a spark. This was applied in the spring.

On 5th April we were walking along the banks of the river Jhelum on our way to meet H.H. the Maharajah of Kashmir, when we met four men carrying a sick person on a string bedstead. We stopped them, to see what was wrong, and saw an emaciated corpse-like form, a man in the collapse stage of cholera.

At that time we had a full hospital with over a hundred in-patients. During the week preceding the outbreak, great crowds of people had flocked in to a Mohammedan fair and hundreds had thronged our waiting-room. On one day alone we had admitted thirty in-patients and performed fifty-three surgical operations. Two patients in the hospital were stricken with cholera and died in a few hours. The others were panic-stricken and in a few hours the hospital was almost empty.

By arrangement with the Superintending Surgeon of the State, who was most helpful, one of us took charge of a large district including the eastern suburbs of the city and outlying villages. And Dr Arthur Neve visited nearly every part of the valley where there was any mortality. On an average there were a hundred deaths a day in the city. In two months the total mortality considerably exceeded ten thousand. Scattered villages, with a good water supply, escaped to a large extent. As usual the cholera marched along the main routes, and every infected water supply became a focus of disease and death.

Of recent years the completion of the Jhelum Valley Road and the greatly increased traffic to and from India have unfortunately made outbreaks of cholera more frequent. In twenty years there have been five serious epidemics with at least forty thousand deaths. The fatal years were 1888, 1892, 1900, 1907 and 1910. Before the year 1900, however, a supply of pure water had been laid on to most parts of the city, and thousands of lives were saved thereby. In 1888 and 1892 Srinagar was a "City of Dreadful Death." "We are looking from the bows of our mat-roofed boat for the first sight of Srinagar, the so-called Venice of the East. The turbid and lazy stream sweeps against the prow, masses of dirty foam, floating straw, dead bodies of dogs, and all the other garbage of a great city. How can one admire the great sweep of snow mountains, the deep azure of the sky, and broad rippling sheet of cloud and sky-reflecting water, when every sense is assailed by things that disgust. Upon one bank stands a neat row of wooden huts. This is a cholera hospital. Upon the other bank the blue smoke curling up from a blazing pile gives atmosphere and distance to the rugged mountains. It is a funeral pyre. And as our boat passes into the city, now and again we meet other boats, each with their burden of death. All traffic seems to be suspended. Shops are closed. Now and again, from some neighbouring barge, we hear the wail of mourners, the shrieks of women as in a torture den, echoed away among the houses on the bank." [1]

Early in the spring of 1907 there was a sharp epidemic of cholera at the west end of the valley. In some of the villages the mortality was appalling. When I arrived in the Lolab in the first week of May, things were quite at their worst. In some houses, one by one all had been attacked, and the last survivor was left with no one to attend and give food and water. The village official who reported the cases had just died. The head-man of the village refused to move out of his house, and panic was universal. Both the State doctors who were working in the district were old Mission Hospital assistants, and they were doing their work well. Having frequently done medical work in the Lolab before, I found that the people were friendly and willing to be treated.

Many of the village springs became veritable death tanks. And sometimes the disease was disseminated as the direct result of superstitious observances. On one occasion, for

[1] Dr A. Neve, *Mission Hospital Reports.*

instance, the Mohammedan priests of a famous shrine made a proclamation that to avert the pestilence, the tank in the courtyard of the sacred edifice should be at once filled with water brought by the worshippers. The people came in their hundreds, each bearing a water-pot which was duly emptied into the tank, some of the water of which was then drunk as a preservative from cholera. Unfortunately the water was infected, and the disastrous outburst of cholera which followed was acknowledged even by the Mohammedans to be obviously due to the work of the previous day.

Both cholera and smallpox are a source of grave danger to Europeans residing in Kashmir. Several have died of cholera.

Until the introduction of general vaccination, practically the whole population of Kashmir contracted smallpox in childhood. The mortality was appalling. From this and other causes fifty per cent. of the children of Kashmir are said to die in infancy. I often wish the opponents of vaccination could be present in our consulting-room to see the melancholy procession, day by day, of those who have lost their sight from smallpox. For this disease is the most frequent cause of total incurable blindness.

Those who are vaccinated, especially if recently so, live with safety and impunity even in the midst of infection. Doctors and nurses enjoy the same immunity as they do in smallpox hospitals at home.

On the other hand, on more than one occasion in our small British community, children, whose vaccination has been omitted, have been singled out by the disease, in one case with fatal result. In contrast to this there has been no case of smallpox, within my memory, in the children of native Christians—a small group, properly vaccinated, under the supervision of the Medical Mission. From time to time European adults, who have neglected re-vaccination, are attacked.

Public vaccination has of recent years been carried on

with a certain measure of efficiency, and with the utmost benefit to the infant population. As might be anticipated, young adults are now, however, occasionally attacked by smallpox. This is, of course, owing to the fact that no adequate provision has been made for their re-vaccination.

Enteric fever is also common in Srinagar. Kashmiri children usually contract it at an early age. Its prevalence constitutes a real danger to European visitors to Kashmir.

Like many other towns with large rivers, Srinagar, in a marvellous way, escaped having plague in a severe form. There was, however, a sharp epidemic in 1903. A man died immediately after his arrival in the mail-cart from India. His body was buried in quicklime. His friends secretly exhumed the corpse in order to re-inter it near a sacred shrine. They were attacked and the disease spread rapidly. It assumed the pneumonic form. And curiously enough there was no associated rat mortality. The authorities took vigorous measures, at first burning down all plague-infected houses. They were, however, compelled to abandon this, owing to popular opposition. The disease gradually died out, after lingering with singular persistence in some isolated villages near the Wular Lake. The mortality, all through, was terrible—over 95 per cent. Kashmiris, who were under European influence, were willing to submit to prophylactic inoculation. No European was attacked by plague.

Modern civilization brings in its train many physical evils. Not the least of these is the multiplication of diseases. The abandonment of open-air life is followed by an enormous increase in the amount of tuberculosis, with its innumerable manifestations. As different trades and occupations are introduced, so the variety of disorders of the skin, the eye, the nervous and other systems becomes multiplied, until now in Europe the number of diseases is almost infinite. In the East we have fewer diseases, but the number of people affected is relatively and actually greater. Infection from want of sanitary precautions plays a great part. Contagion is responsible for many of the local diseases which are rampant—such as ophthalmia, scaldhead and the itch. A peculiar form of malignant disease, called "Kangri burn cancer," is due to the universal use of portable braziers.

In other respects the diseases of Kashmir are very much the same as those met with in Europe.

18. CENTRAL TOWER, MISSION HOSPITAL.

CHAPTER VII

THE MISSION HOSPITAL

New Buildings—A Beautiful Prospect—A Crowd of Sick People—Reclaimed—Items of Expenditure—A Provident System—A Walk round the Wards—Mohammedans and Hindus—Types of Patients—A Little Sufferer—St Luke's Chapel—The Relief of Lepers.

Many are the pains of life ; I need not stay
To count them ; there is no one but hath felt
Some of them—though unequally they fall—
But of all good gifts, ever hath been health
Counted the first, and the loss of it to be
The hardest thing to bear. . . .

H. E. HAMILTON KING.

THE long western ridge of the Takht-i-Suleiman is prolonged into a picturesque grassy spur which used to be crowned by an old fort and is known as the Rustum Gaddi. On the south side of this are the high reddish-yellow cliffs of a stone quarry. On the north side, a hundred feet above the level of the valley, in a commanding position, is the Mission Hospital. This has been entirely rebuilt since 1888. In those days it was all lath and plaster with mud walls and mud floors. At the present time, the new buildings are most picturesque, with their towers, broad verandahs, red roofs and gables extending for nearly a quarter of a mile along the hillside, embowered in the spring in almond blossom, or in the summer showing pretty glimpses of form and colour between the masses of varied foliage (Plate 18).

"From the upper verandahs, the prospect is indeed beautiful. Sparkling a hundred feet below is the clear flowing water of the network of canals joining the lake, the city and the European quarters. Away over the tops of the tall poplars we catch a glimpse of the airy pinnacles of the city mosques; beyond these the hazy blue outlines of rolling hills, over which, on the south and west, are the noble serrated ridges of the Pir Panjal melting away in the distance till they blend with the sky.

"To the north, but a few miles away, rise masses of rocky mountains, enclosing in their grand sweep the Dal Lake and a maze of gardens, orchards and willow-hidden waterways, dominated by the bare red slopes and fortified crest of the isolated fort hill.

"Within the circle of that snow range dwell half a million souls, for whom the red cross flag, waving from the hospital hill, has a message of 'peace and goodwill among men.' And if that message has yet to be intelligibly delivered in its fulness to hundreds of thousands of these, yet to how many has the goodwill been practically manifested?" How many thousands were relieved in the dark and terrible years of famine, earthquake and cholera! Year by year, too, thousands of sick people, with many varied ailments, throng to the hospital for relief. Since Dr Elmslie first founded the work in 1865, far more people have applied to the Medical Mission for relief than there are now inhabitants in the valley. During the last ten years alone, over four hundred thousand visits have been paid, and 14,500 in-patients have been treated in the hospital wards.

At the east end of the hospital, high up on the hillside, is a large building with a central tower. This is the out-patient department, with a commodious waiting-room, consulting-rooms, dispensary, bacteriological laboratory and operation-rooms fitted with all the appliances necessary for the efficient carrying on of an extensive medical and surgical work. On a busy day in the summer, before midday, little groups of people may be seen gradually collecting, sitting in the shade of the trees, waiting for the doors to open. An old blind man will be brought up on a rough mountain pony. Four men may be seen staggering up the hill carrying on a bedstead a man with a broken leg. This little pro-

19. TYPES OF PATIENTS.
(Hindu, Sikh, Punjábi, and Mohammedan.)

cession with a sedan-chair, with the red curtains flapping in the breeze, is accompanying a "parda" woman of the better classes. The old man with hardly any clothes on, and his body smeared with white ashes, is a Hindu Sadhu from India. Look at the elaborate caste marks on his face! The little group of men with sturdy ponies and long coats, like wadded dressing-gowns, are from Yarkand in Central Asia. See how fair they are, and their cheeks are quite red. They are making the pilgrimage to Mecca. The sprightly little man behind is a Goorkha soldier. His home is Nepal. He is probably "orderly" to some officer. How many creeds and nations are represented here (Plate 19). Kashmiri Mohammedans, men and women, in their dirty gowns, predominate; but here also may be seen herdsmen from the hills, tall, pale and melancholy-looking, and usually clothed in dark blue. Kashmiri Hindus and their families may be seen side by side with Buddhists from Ladákh. From many remote districts around, patients come—sometimes journeying for days and weeks across passes. "Many are the pains of life." Here we see some people disfigured by large goitres, others crippled with chronic rheumatism, and some with their faces so marred by disease as to impel them to keep them hidden from sight. The blind, with cataract or ophthalmia, the halt and maimed, paralysed or sufferers from diseases of bones or joints, the cancer-stricken, those afflicted with dropsy, lepers, and crowds with every variety of surgical ailment, toil up the steps to the waiting-room as the midday gun is fired. The room is soon packed, the patients sitting on the floor, and the door is closed. The babel of voices subsides as the doctor comes in and reads some appropriate passage from the New Testament, which he then explains in simple language, and endeavours to apply directly to the need of those before him. This is listened to attentively. Here and there one audibly assents. There is no feeling of antagonism. Many are doubtless languid or indifferent. But most feel that the combination of spiritual with physical ministration is fitting, and is it not what they have been accustomed to in their own religion? At the close of the address a short prayer is offered. It is by no means unfrequent for many of those present to associate themselves in this by saying Amen, like our good Wesleyan friends, at the close of each petition.

One by one the patients, summoned by the ringing of a small bell, pass into the next room, where they are examined and prescribed for by the surgeon on duty.

One day I was seated in the consulting-room, engaged in seeing the out-patients, when in marched a funny little object. It was a little six-year-old girl, with unkempt hair, one ragged and scant garment, and a sharp, intelligent face. There was no one with her, and the most careful inquiry failed to elicit any information about her home or parents. When asked, "Where do you come from?" she pointed west. Interrogated further, she stated that she had slept at the roadside the previous night. About her origin we could, however, ascertain nothing. Like Topsy, she appeared to have growed.

That the Mission Hospital was the best place to which she could have come was quite certain, for she was suffering from a terrible deformity, which quite marred her beauty. Her head was bound down to the left side by an enormous scar, resulting from a previous burn, so that the cheek was almost in contact with the tip of the shoulder, to which it was firmly attached.

How this forlorn little maiden happened to stray into our consulting-room, whether it was her own idea, or whether she had been directed to us, we have never found out.

We admitted her, and in the course of a day or two an extensive surgical operation was performed. As the result of this, her condition was much improved, and after careful attention, in the course of two or three months, it was evident that although her head was curiously tilted to one side, the original deformity was largely removed. And what was to be done now? Were we to turn out the poor little vessel to take its chance amongst all the brazen and the iron and the earthenware pots which are floating down the current of life? If so, what about the shallows and the rapids and the falls. No; we felt that she was sent to us to be cared for, and so with the aid of kind friends, we sent her to a Christian boarding school, with the hope that under good influences she might grow up to be a Christian, not only in name but in word and deed.

For some hours the work of prescribing for the patients goes on. Many have wounds which require dressing. Splints have to be applied and medicines distributed. The surgical work is often very heavy. Twelve major and forty minor operations may be performed in a single day. Sometimes as many as 400 patients are seen in one day.

It is often a little difficult to grasp the significance of figures. Four hundred patients, if they stood in single file, would reach a quarter of a mile. The total number of patients who attend in one year, if they stood two and two, rather close together, would extend to a distance of 16 miles. About 25 miles of bandage are used annually and 18,000 lbs. weight of medicine. The amount of rice supplied annually gratis to patients is fourteen tons, and of milk about twenty-five tons.

It would be quite impossible to carry on this extensive work without the large amount of assistance and support which we receive from a great number of friends. First among these must be mentioned our colleague, Dr Harold Rawlence, who has absolutely identified himself with the work of the Mission Hospital. I have already referred to the most important and valued work done by Miss Neve as Superintendent of Nursing. To this we owe much of the efficiency of the hospital. There is also a large band of assistants, some of them, like Dr Wilson, our house-surgeon, Indian Christians, and others Hindus, who have, however, been trained in the Mission School. These form a staff of willing helpers. We could not do the work without them. If many hands do not make light work, they at least make it easier.

Owing, too, to the generosity of many friends, both in India and at home, most of the beds are endowed, and sufficient funds are received to enable us, with the aid of fees received from medical practice, to meet all the hospital expenses, without any grant from the Church Missionary Society or from the Kashmir State.

The annual cost of each bed in the hospital is about £10. In the London hospitals it averages £90 per bed. The chief saving in Kashmir is effected on salaries, cost of labour and of provisions. But economy in surgical dressings and apparatus is an important factor. For instance, instead of medicated cotton-wool at a rupee per pound, we substitute to a large extent muslin bags full of sawdust and disinfected in a high pressure steam sterilizer before use. The sawdust costs about one anna for 10 lbs.

India owes a great debt of gratitude to the Government for its splendid system of civil hospitals. But hitherto, adequate provision has not been made to obviate the free supply of medical advice and medicines to large numbers of those who could quite well afford and ought to pay for them.

The vast majority of our hospital patients are poor, and they receive attendance and medicines absolutely free and without reference to religion. One claim is sufficient, that they are ill and need relief. So also in the wards of the hospital, patients are treated, clothed and nursed gratuitously.

To meet, however, the needs of the increasing class of those who are well-to-do and seek medical aid, we have erected a block of pay-wards, for admission to which a suitable charge is made. Also in the out-patient department, those who are willing to pay for advice and medicine are admitted by a separate door, on the payment of a fee, which is fixed on a sliding scale, according to the income of the applicant. For this a receipt is given, which is used as a ticket entitling the possessor to private entrance to the consulting-room.

20. UPPER VERANDAH DOWNES' WARD.

Leaving the out-patient department, we descend a long flight of steps. The westering sun is shining brightly and lighting up the wards with its warm orange glow. The air is fragrant with the perfume of countless roses which may be seen along the borders of the red paths. Beyond lies the trimly-kept garden with its gay flower-beds, well-clipped evergreen shrubs, and soft green velvety turf. We walk through the wards. The patients seem to live in the open air. In the broad verandahs there are lines and lines of polished black iron bedsteads, occupied by patients, most of whom, too, are evidently convalescing if we may judge by their cheerful aspect and bright manners. Their white clothes and happy faces, the scarlet blankets and neat grey boards with the name at the head of each bed in red letters, the pale green walls and mirror-like floors all combine to make a pretty picture which is enhanced by the feeling of underlying utility (Plate 20).

Altogether there is accommodation for 150 patients. Sometimes we have more, and beds have to be made up on the floor. It is very interesting to go round the hospital and see the large number of inmates. More than a hundred different towns and villages may be represented. Many of the patients have visitors or relatives sitting by them, and these are allowed to come at all times, so that there may sometimes be more than two hundred people in the hospital. Most of these are Mohammedans, but there are a good many Hindus, and a sprinkling of other nationalities, Punjabis, Sikhs, Tibetans and Gujars from the mountains. As a rule we are fortunate in being able to make ourselves understood to the great majority, for most know either Kashmiri or a little Urdu.

There are always a good many children in the hospital. At first they are often absolutely terrified, but they soon get to know us and become cheerful and even gay. Toys given by English children in Srinagar, or sent out from England, are greatly appreciated.

One little fellow in the "Plymouth" bed is only three years old. He was brought in with a very large tumour of the leg. During the operation it was found that the only chance for him was to amputate at the knee. Usually such a decision causes a terrible hubbub amongst the friends, and often permission is refused. But in this case the relations, although naturally greatly distressed, made no difficulties. We found that they had been in before with another patient, who had recovered from a very serious illness. The boy is now convalescent. He is hugging a large tambourine with a cat's head painted on it, and also a tin trumpet, and is happy all day. When I go into the ward he smiles all over his face, and salutes by putting his hand to his forehead.

In the "Croydon Lay Workers' Union" bed there is now a fat little boy of five, whose foot and leg were terribly burnt some weeks ago. He has had several skin grafts applied and is slowly healing. Another child in the "Norbiton" bed is suffering from disease of the shin-bone and knee-joint. His joint was twice tapped, but eventually a more extensive operation had to be performed for the removal of all the disease, and he is now convalescent. He has been very good and patient over it all. Next to him, in the "Heylyn Platt" cot, is a little fellow with hip-joint disease. He has a large wooden horse to play with. Its tail has come off and it has sustained various casualties, but he does not mind.

As we walk through the hospital we are struck by the commonness of certain ailments. There are nearly a dozen people who have been operated upon for kangri burn cancer. The kangri is the fire-basket, which the people carry under their clothes to keep themselves warm. All their lives, from early childhood, they burn themselves with these things; and when they get old, cancer is apt to follow from the prolonged irritation.

The women's wards are in the "Sir Pertabh Singh Pavilion" (named after H.H. the Maharajah of Kashmir, who formally opened it in 1893). Here there are nine or ten women who have been operated upon for in-turned eyelashes. They were rapidly losing their sight, but will now steadily improve and regain vision. In the "Lloyd Edwards" bed is a patient for whom an important operation was required for a very large tumour. She is almost well. In the "Gertrude" bed is an old lady with ankle-joint disease, who is being treated by modern methods, and is slowly improving. We trust we shall now be able to save the limb. The "Nazareth" bed is occupied by a young woman with disease of one of the bones of the arm. She is always bright and pleasant and is doing well. There is an elderly woman in the "Kensington" bed with a severe burn of the elbow. She fell down in a faint as the result of insufficient food and the severe cold in the winter and was burnt by her kangri. She is an old patient and was "in" years ago for cataract of both eyes and then received her sight.

These wards are under the special charge of Miss Neve, the Superintendent of Nursing, who also teaches the patients. Some of the younger ones are quite good at learning and repeating texts, but the women as a whole are not very attentive listeners. There are, however, fairly frequent exceptions.

In the wards of the hospital we obtain a glimpse into the better side of Kashmir life. Many of the patients are villagers. Supposing a little child falls ill, and is brought in, he is often accompanied by quite a number of relatives. Some of these usually remain for a few days, and as they become accustomed to our ways and methods they grow more and more friendly. Sometimes, in rotation, nearly every member of a family will come to take turn in watching by and nursing a little patient. The father goes back to his fields, his place is taken by the mother. She, in turn, is too much needed at home, and has reluctantly to leave, handing over charge, perhaps, to an old grandmother. Sometimes confidence is so far gained that the friends will commend the child to our care for days or weeks, ever and anon putting in an appearance to see how things are going on.

Zuni was a little Kashmiri girl nine years old. She had gone through a good deal of trouble at home. She hardly remembered her father, who died long ago. Her mother's health was very bad, and poor little Zuni had been left to fend for herself. When her leg became swollen and painful, the outlook seemed very bad. Her mother was too poor to pay for the attendance of native doctors, which was perhaps just as well for Zuni, for they would very likely have bled her and given her poisonous drugs containing mercury, till her gums became spongy and her teeth loose. A neighbour suggested their going to the Mission Hospital, but they were afraid, because they knew of a boy in the next street whose leg had been cut off there. It is true that the boy was well and happy and loud in his praises of the hospital as a place where they got lots to eat and every one was kind. But the possibility of her leg being cut off was too dreadful! Zuni would rather die first. So they postponed it and put it off, but then the leg got very sore and she could not walk at all, and began to get very pale and thin. At last they hired a boat and started off. Presently they saw a long row of buildings, with several towers, on the side of a hill, and up above was a white flag with a red cross on it. They were told that this was the Mission Hospital, and Zuni was lifted out of the boat by her aunt and carried up the hill to a large room where there was a great crowd of people. She counted 150. They were all sitting on the ground. Then the doctor came in and Zuni was very frightened, until she saw that he had nothing more dreadful than a book in his hand. He sat down, read to the people from the book, which he said was the Gospel, and then talked to them, and Zuni was surprised to find that she could understand something of what he said, and that he was telling the people of a great

Prophet, who went about doing good and healing the sick and who gave His own life in order to save men from sin.

Then after the doctor had finished and gone out, she heard a little bell ring and ring; and each time it rang, one of the sick people got up and went out of the big room and was lost to sight. And Zuni wondered whether they were all having arms and legs cut off, but thought not, as she did not hear any cry except a small and naughty baby, which was evidently very cross, and which was smacked by its mother, which did not improve its temper. Presently her turn came and Zuni was taken into the next room and the doctor looked at her leg and said she must have something to send her to sleep and then he would put the leg right. Then her aunt began to cry, and she cried too, and felt sure she was going to have her leg cut off and be killed. And they took her into a very bright room and put her on a shiny table and gave her some strange sweet stuff on a towel to smell, and she felt the whole room whirl round, and the noise in her ears reminded her of the great flood, when the stream near their home became a roaring torrent and nearly swept them all away. Then she seemed to hear far-away voices, which appeared to get louder; and she was just going to implore them not to do anything to her, when to her surprise she was told that it was all finished. She then fell asleep and when she awoke she was in a nice clean, comfortable bed, with white sheets and red blankets and such a soft pillow. And in the next bed to her she was surprised to see another little girl of about her own age, whose name was Khotani, and who said her home was in the mountains. They were soon great friends and Khotani told her that she had been in the hospital for two months and was getting better, and it was a jolly place, and the Miss Sahibs were very kind. And she showed her such a nice doll and told her stories about life in the mountains, among the pines and snows, and all about her pet lamb and her father's buffaloes. And the Miss Sahib used to come and read to them and talk to them, and both Zuni and Khotani learned texts and liked to hear about the little Child who was born in Bethlehem, and about the angel who came to tell good news to the shepherds. One day Zuni had a beautiful Japanese doll given to her, and it made her very happy. And a large musical-box used to be brought into the ward sometimes and it played beautiful tunes and she was so pleased. Zuni remained some months in the hospital, and began quite to look upon it as her home.

Many of the patients come a good deal under the influence of Christian teaching. But when they return to their homes, too often the weight of public opinion is brought to bear against the teaching which they have heard. We are doing perhaps more than we can guess, even in our sanguine moments, towards leavening and modifying that public opinion. Although nominally assenting to much of Christian doctrine, the general feeling of the Mohammedan community is naturally very strongly against a change of religion. The Hindus, on the other hand, have, of course, still less in common with Christianity, and their whole religious thought seems to be on quite a different plane. In the abstract, the Hindu is more tolerant than the Mohammedan, but in reality he is not one whit more so, if any member of his community should show the desire of becoming a Christian.

It seems, and is, a bold enterprise for a mere handful of Christians, brought up in a distant country and of an alien race, with different manners, customs, sentiments and habits, to try to bring the people of a country like Kashmir to believe in Christ, with all that this belief (taken in the Christian sense) implies. The difficulty is not diminished by the fact that the lives of many Christians, with whom the people come into contact, carry with them very little Christian influence. It is increased by the want of religious freedom and toleration in Kashmir. Hindus and Mohammedans are seldom backward in applauding the impartiality exhibited by the Government of India in all matters of religion, but they do not imitate it. The convert to Christianity in Kashmir has to endure a storm of persecution. He becomes an outcast from his family and an object of contempt and hatred to his former co-religionists. He usually loses his means of livelihood, and is ostracized by his friends and neighbours. Yet these very difficulties accentuate the importance of the work. The evangelization of the world has from the earliest days had to encounter persecution, hatred, intolerance and scorn. Time after time it has triumphed, and by the grace of God it will do so in Kashmir, but we must have patience.

"Among those who appear interested, in the wards, are certain types. One is the old soldier who has served under British officers, or the Indian servant who has been long in the employ of a kind master. Perhaps little may have been said to them about religion, but they have seen something of its effect on the English character, and when spoken to personally, under the solemnizing influence of a severe illness, they respond to it. Let me give two examples. S. K. had served thirteen years in a Punjab regiment and had fought under the British flag in Egypt as well as in Afghanistan and on the frontier. His home is 100 miles west of this, but he had heard of the hospital, and when other treatment failed to relieve his dropsy resulting from heart disease, he travelled up here, on horseback, accompanied by two or three relatives. Tapping and other treatment relieved him considerably, and he was very grateful for all the personal attention shown him, and was ready to talk about his former experiences. As time went on, his heart seemed touched by the thought of God's love, and he spoke of Christ as the Saviour. He not only listened himself, but made others do so, and any Hindustani-speaking patients in the wards would join with him in responding during an address or prayer. His improvement was not maintained altogether, and at last he reluctantly started for home, appearing much affected at parting. Of such an one surely the hope may be expressed that there will be a happier meeting above."

"P. K. was brought to us in an extreme state of weakness

from an incurable disease. I had known him as the trustworthy henchman of a gentleman living here. We could only relieve him a little, and stave off the end by a few days. But he was thankful, and asked me to pray with him. I broke it to him gently that he could not hope to see his master and mistress again, as they would not be back for some weeks. We talked of the life beyond, and he listened to the words of Christ as if they gave him comfort. And he who gave comfort to that dying Mohammedan will not, we may be sure, refuse to intercede for him at the Mercy Seat on high."

"Another type is the devout old villager, perhaps a Mullah or Pir, who may have come from a distance to have his eyes operated on for cataract. Some men of this kind seem really religious, not mere formalists; they listen well, and often comment briefly on the teaching, and the more spiritual this is, the more they appear to appreciate it. Pleasant as it is to talk to these, they do not readily receive any new doctrine. The Atonement of Christ does not seem to appeal to them, though the story of the Resurrection and Ascension does so, and still more the doctrine of Christ as the Great Intercessor. But saint worship in Kashmir has reached such lengths that perhaps they believe as much about their 'Pirs' as we claim for our Divine Master. One or two of the more educated villagers have expressed much interest, but we have lost sight of them lately. One from the west of the valley read the Gospels and some tracts, and was at first a little argumentative, but later on he openly, before some Mohammedans, said he was not one of them, for he was a Christian."

"A different type to this is the lad, possibly suffering from bone or joint disease, who likes to get hold of a book and to hear something novel. The interest is often very superficial to start with, but if it can be followed up, may make a deep impression."[1]

At the foot of the Rustum Gaddi Hill and at the east end of the hospital garden, opening on to the main road to the

[1] Dr A. Neve, *Mission Hospital Reports.*

city, is the pretty little chapel of St Luke. It is built of grey stone, and the windows, cornices, mouldings and interior lining are of red brick. The church is cruciform, with an apsidal chancel, on either side of which are brass memorial tablets to Dr Elmslie and Mr K. B. Thomas and to Miss Petrie and Miss F. Butler, the first lady medical missionary to Kashmir. The reredos is a fine piece of carving in walnut wood. In the north transept there is also a tablet in memory of Miss Robinson, who for eight years rendered most faithful service as nursing sister.

Gothic arches of timber support the roof, the inside of which is ceiled with a beautiful parqueterie, peculiar to Kashmir, and known as *khatmband*, thin slips of pine wood pieced together with great skill to form a bold geometrical pattern.

Near the end of the nave at the entrance, a carved screen stretches across the church, behind which are the seats for Mohammedans and Hindus.

St Luke's Chapel was dedicated by the Bishop of Lahore on 12th September 1896, in the presence of a large congregation, partly European and partly native. Among the natives, Kashmiri, Punjabi, Pathan and Bengali were represented. This ceremony marked an epoch in the Mission.

From time to time we have the joy of witnessing in this building the admission of members to the Christian Church.

One of the last was Lass Sheikh, a leper, who had long been interested in Christian teaching, and who had been living a quiet and consistent life in the leper hospital. At the same time a boy, the son of one of the other lepers, was, at his own desire and with his father's consent, admitted to the visible church. The service, which was conducted by the Rev. F. E. Lucey, was most impressive, as first one and then the other in the presence of the congregation confessed his faith in Christ, and promised to fight faithfully under His banner—a pledge which, in Kashmir, is no empty form, but a veritable taking up of the cross.

In past years many inquirers, dreading the persecution which is inevitable in Kashmir, have fled to the Punjab, where some have been baptized.

Of those who have been baptized in Kashmir, several have sooner or later apostatized. Kashmiri Christians require very strong faith and an unusually strong character to withstand the depressing effect of the constant disabilities to which they are exposed, owing to their religious belief.

The whole strength of popular prejudice, of caste and of officialdom is against a change of religion. But all these are as impotent to stay the change which is coming surely and slowly over India, as was Canute to stem the rising tide.

Education is making strides, and the future is bright with the hopes of enlightenment and intellectual freedom. The true power and beneficence of Christianity are becoming increasingly acknowledged.

A Mission Hospital is a " moral text-book," which can be read and appreciated by the most illiterate. And we are right in revealing our sources of inspiration. We have a message, the message of peace and goodwill to men through the Saviour Christ. Day by day, week by week, these good tidings of great joy have been told. Oftentimes, I fear, they have appeared foolishness to the hearers. History repeats itself. For the pantheistic Greek substitute the Hindu, for the monotheistic Jew take the Mohammedan, and to the one " Christ Crucified " is still a stumbling-block, and to the other foolishness. Nevertheless we believe with St Paul that to those who receive Him, Christ is the Power of God and the Wisdom of God. During the past years many Kashmiris have apparently listened to this message with devoutness and thankfulness.

Twenty years ago a visitor walking round the Kashmir Mission Hospital would have found one building occupied exclusively by lepers. At that time the hospital wards were built of lath and plaster, with earthen floors, and the accommodation for the lepers was perhaps the worst of all. From sixty to eighty lepers used to come to us annually as out-patients. Of these, at the most, twelve could be admitted. About this time there was a wave of interest in lepers. Father Damien had recently died of the disease, and the Prince of Wales's Fund had been started. It was a specially suitable opportunity for pressing a request that we should be allowed to build a separate hospital for lepers in Kashmir. This request was favourably received by H.H. the Maharajah, who most kindly granted us an admirable site of about twelve acres, on a peninsula projecting into the Dal Lake, and he allotted to us a sum of about £300 for the erection of the first buildings, and one year's maintenance. This was the commencement of the present Kashmir State Hospital. Accommodation was provided for thirty patients, and in the year 1891, the first year of the work, we had in the summer months an average of twenty as our leper family. While looking after their temporal needs we were glad to be able to tell them of a Home where sin and disease do not enter in, and where there is no more sorrow but joy for evermore.

The number of patients increased year by year, and the thirty beds proved insufficient. In 1894 a small block was erected to hold eight more, and again in 1895 a second extra ward for ten more lepers had to be erected. Since that time, addition after addition has been made to provide for the constantly growing need. In 1899 there were sixty-five patients in the institution. In 1911 the number had reached one hundred. The hospital now is quite one of the show places of Kashmir. It is surrounded on three sides by the blue waters of the lake, and there is a wonderful panorama of snow mountains in every direction to which the eye is turned. The building consists of nine separate lines. Most of these have red-tiled roofs, and they are provided with verandahs. In the three last blocks which have been added, there are five rooms each. Every room has two windows and a little fireplace, and holds two lepers. The floors have been tiled, and ample ventilation provided. In the garden around are hundreds of young fruit trees which we have planted, and we also raise crops of wheat, barley, Indian corn and linseed. The field work is not, however, done by the lepers.

In Kashmir there is no compulsory segregation of lepers. Those who come to the hospital do so voluntarily, and stay just as long as they like. For this reason it has been found difficult to develop industrial work amongst them. It is important that those who are well enough should have some occupation. They are therefore expected to keep their own rooms clean; and odd jobs such as grass-cutting, white-washing, path-making and so on are encouraged. There is also a little school for the children (Plate 21). Most of the lepers come from hill districts around the valley of Kashmir. Many of them belong to the herdsman class. Leprosy is not hereditary. It appears to be propagated by a limited contagion among those who live in crowded huts and under insanitary conditions. There are two chief types of the disease. In one of these there are pale, leprous patches, with loss of sensation. This form affects fingers and toes, which drop off, and it appears to correspond more closely with the leprosy mentioned in the Bible than the other form. The second form, the so-called tubercular leprosy, is far more disfiguring. The body is covered with lumps, and, as these are very numerous on the face, the patients' features are distorted and sometimes look quite leonine. In many, the eyes are attacked and incurable blindness follows only too often. Advanced cases are turned out of their homes and people refuse to eat with them, so their condition is very sad. The less marked cases often continue to live in their villages, and they are a source of danger to others. I remember once when travelling in a mountainous part of Kashmir, going to a cottage and asking for some milk. A man brought me some in his bowl. I was just about to drink it, when, glancing at the man, I saw that he was a leper. There are undoubted risks when lepers are mixed with the population, living, sleeping and eating with healthy people.

Photo by] [*G. W. Possnet.*

21. LITTLE SCHOLARS AT THE LEPER HOSPITAL.

It will at once be perceived that the larger the number ot lepers in the hospital, the better will it fulfil its intention; and the longer every leper can be retained in the institution the better for himself and the rest of the population. The treatment is chiefly palliative. But many of the lepers improve very much, and in some the disease appears to become after a time completely arrested. Food, clothing, bedding, in fact all that they need, is supplied to the lepers; and as funds admit we are gradually furnishing the whole hospital with first-rate iron bedsteads.

The spiritual work in the leper hospital has been up-hill, and in some respects it affords a means of estimating the difficulty of the work in Kashmir, and the apparent slowness of progress. In the leper hospital the patients owe practically everything to Christian work. In their own villages most of them are outcasts, although the people give them alms. The contrast in the leper hospital must be very striking to them. Here they have abundant food and many comforts, with cosy little rooms and firewood in the winter. Their wounds are dressed daily, and a friendly interest is taken in them. When we go to this hospital, after visiting all the patients, we gather them together and read a portion of Scripture, following it with simple explanation or a short evangelistic address. Attendance at this service is voluntary. In the summer, nearly all come: in the winter, the number drops to thirty or forty. The patients listen with attention. They are not good at answering questions; many of them seem to be afraid lest that should be taken by the others as an indication of an intention of becoming Christians. From time to time, however, some have professed their faith, and have been baptized. These have all been subject to a measure of persecution from the other lepers, who promptly refuse to eat with them, and object to live in the same room, and not infrequently show much bitterness. And yet the very people who act in this way often say Amen quite fervently at the close of the prayer with which our service is ended. The fact is that they are ready to assent to a good deal of Christian teaching, but object to baptism, because they realize that a baptized person is no longer one of the great Mohammedan brotherhood, and is therefore from their standpoint a renegade.

The first to become a Christian in the present leper hospital was K. K. He is intelligent and independent, and certainly the best of the lepers. In the first instance he was influenced largely through reading a copy of the New Testament which was given to him.

There is still a tendency for the leper hospital work to grow and increase. Before long I have no doubt that we shall be able to accommodate more than 100 lepers in the institution. It is interesting to know that all this work is, owing to the enlightenment and liberality of the Maharajah of Kashmir, carried on without any charge whatever upon the funds of the Church Missionary Society. If there were no Christians at all, the work would nevertheless be interesting and encouraging, for is it not a literal carrying-out of the command to "heal the sick . . . and say unto them, the Kingdom of God is come nigh unto you"? And if many of the lepers are somewhat unresponsive and their gratitude is not always conspicuous, do we not know of ten lepers who were actually completely restored to health, and yet of whom only one stranger returned to give thanks? Who can say that some of these lepers, taking all their circumstances and the heavy handicap of disease into consideration, may not be really nearer the Kingdom than many Christians, who, enjoying health and the innumerable privileges of a Christian environment, with all that this means, are nevertheless content to live lives of luxury and ease, unmindful of the White Man's Burden, and the great claim of Christian opportunity, which calls us all to work while it is yet day?

CHAPTER VIII

VILLAGE LIFE

Forced Labour—Land Settlement—Rice Cultivation—Sericulture—Village Occupations—Field Work—Horticulture—Apiculture—Autumn and Winter—Some Common Birds.

THE villages of Kashmir are full of human interest as we study the people in their natural environment.

The chief village population is found all round the valley on the higher ground which shelves up to the mountains, on the slopes below the foot-hills, the deltas of the tributary valleys and the sides of the *karewahs*. Here enormous areas of terraced rice-fields are to be found, stretching from the alluvial plain up to the base of the mountains. And as we go a little higher we find whole slopes covered with maize. The flat tops of the *karewahs* are used especially for wheat, barley, mustard and linseed, early crops which come to maturity before the scorching heat of summer parches the soil.

The life of Kashmir depends upon its agriculturists. The population of the Kashmir Province is 1,295,203, and of these probably more than a million are engaged in agriculture. In olden days the interests of the villagers were largely subordinated to those of the inhabitants of the city of Srinagar, many of whom were influential and all of whom were more immediately under the eye of the rulers.

Rice for the city was taken from the villagers at low rates. They were liable to frequent calls for forced labour. Every year the levy of coolies for Gilgit placed in the hands of the Tehsildars (the district magistrates) great powers of oppression. And from the chief of the local administration down to the humblest peon of the Tehsil this was an unfailing source of income. Meanwhile, the poor and friendless, or those who had incurred the wrath of the authorities, were seized and sent off on the hated task of carrying loads a thirteen days' journey, over rough mountain tracks to Gilgit. Their condition was indeed little better than that of slaves.

"In May 1888 I was on cholera duty in Islamabad. Just as the epidemic was reaching its height, and hundreds were dying every day in all the districts around, a levy of 5000 or more coolies was called for. The villagers were almost distracted with fear. Who would do all the agricultural work? What would happen, during their long absence, to their wives and children? To what perils of pestilence and inclemency of weather would they themselves be exposed in the crowded bivouacs and snowy passes of the deadly Gilgit district? I was present at a sort of farewell service on a *maidan* outside Islamabad, when nearly 1000 men were starting. And when they took leave of the friends who had accompanied them so far, loud was the sobbing of some, fervid the demeanour of all as, led by the mullah, they intoned their prayers and chanted some of their special Ramzan penitential psalms. Braver men might well have been agitated at such a time. It is certain that cholera clung to the camp, and that unburied corpses of hundreds of these poor 'begáris' marked the whole line of march from Srinagar to Bunji." [1]

In the year 1882 the State tried the remarkable experiment of auctioning the villages for revenue purposes. The purchasers in many cases bid amounts which were absurdly greater than the value of the village revenue, and after wringing all they could out of the unhappy villagers they absconded without paying the State a single rupee. This was bad enough. But to aggravate it the State actually professed to regard the sum offered at the auction as the real

[1] A. Neve, *Mission Hospital Reports.*

22. A TYPICAL KASHMIRI COTTAGE.
(To the right is the little granary.)

value of the village tax, and year by year put pressure upon the unfortunate cultivators with a view to realizing this fictitious revenue!

The great land settlement, initiated by Sir Andrew Wingate in 1887, and carried through by Sir Walter Lawrence from 1889-1895, changed all this, and from that time the condition of the villagers has been one of increasing prosperity. Two among many evidences of this are the large areas of new land being annually brought under cultivation, and the numerous shops, which are springing up in the villages, stocked with cotton piece goods and other luxuries or necessities of civilization.

The abolition of the old method of a special low rate for rice, fixed by Government, was, however, effected too abruptly. It had been going on for generations, and the life of the poorer inhabitants of Srinagar was largely dependent upon cheap food thus obtained. When the market was thrown open in 1902, the price of rice rushed up to more than fourfold, and thousands in the city were threatened by starvation. The Government was compelled to readjust the situation and for a time to make grants of cheaper grain to those who were really poor.

Kashmiri villages are conspicuous in the landscape. There is usually a group of chenar trees, with light grey trunks, mottled with pale yellow, and massive curved limbs, with dense foliage forming dark green masses in summer and brilliant splashes of light red in the late autumn. Close by are two or three lofty poplars and lines of young saplings, bordering orchards of pear, apple and apricot, or market gardens enclosed by wattle fences. Mounds covered with large purple and white irises, brilliant and fragrant in the sunshine, mark the sites of the old village graveyards, and the hamlet itself shows as a collection of large high-pitched, straw-thatched gables, peeping out from among the mulberry trees (Plate 22).

These homesteads embowered in trees are surrounded

by thousands of acres of arable land, terraced squares and crescents of rice-field, irrigated from small channels.

Rice ripens up to an altitude of about 7000 feet. It is the staple crop of Kashmir. There are at least sixty different varieties with distinct names; but there are two broad divisions, viz., white and red. The former is considered greatly superior.

The successful cultivation of rice entails enormous labour. First of all the fields have to be constructed in terraces so as to allow of effective irrigation. Channels have to be dug for the distribution of the water. It is essential, when the rice has been sown or planted out from the nurseries, that the soil shall never again get dry. The weeding alone is a tremendous task. Rows of peasants may be seen standing in mud and water, bent down, scooping out all the adventitious plants and grasses, and plastering mud round the stalks of the young rice plants. This goes on day after day under a hot sun, and the fields have to be carefully and completely weeded no less than four times a year. Where, however, the rice plants have been transferred from nurseries, instead of being sown broadcast, twice is sufficient. This special weeding is called *khushába.*

The Kashmiri is an absolute expert in rice cultivation, and unless early frost steps in, continuous rain at harvest-time, or one of the disastrous inundations to which Kashmir is so liable, there is usually a splendid harvest.

Throughout the valley there is very extensive irrigation. The water can be taken off at great heights from the tributary valleys, and there are also a large number of springs. The distribution is very wide and is said to be conducted on a system introduced by the Moghuls.

In and around Srinagar and the larger towns and villages lift irrigation is also carried on largely by means of a long pole acting as a lever and working on a pivot upon a cross-piece resting on two uprights, or on the forked branches of a tree. The short end of the pole carries a large stone as a counterpoise, and on to the long end like the line of a fishing-rod hangs a thick rope with an earthenware bucket attached. This is rapidly lowered into the river or well by pulling on the rope and dragging down the end of the pole. When this is released the weight of the stone raises the bucket which, as it reaches the level of the ground, is emptied into a long boat-shaped tray of wood which acts like a funnel and conducts the water in the required direction. This form of irrigation is especially useful for market gardens. All the land really belongs to the State. But hereditary rights of occupancy have been granted to cultivators who pay their taxes regularly. They are not, however, allowed under any circumstances to sell or mortgage their land. This rule saves them from the clutches of the Hindu banias and middlemen. And if it is necessary for a villager to raise money, he can usually do it in advance on his standing crops.

A certain number of high officers and privileged persons, such as the Mian Rajputs, the clan of H.H. the Maharajah, hold estates in Kashmir, which are revenue free and not under the control of the Forest Department. These are called Jagirs.

The land revenue actually collected in Kashmir in 1890 was twelve and a half lakhs of rupees (£83,715). This is about what it was in the time of the Emperor Akhbar.

Of recent years, however, although the *taxation* has been reduced from fifty to thirty per cent. of the total crops of the cultivators, the land *revenue* has greatly increased, and it is now more than half as much again as it was in 1890.

Entering the village, we usually find a broad track with grassy borders bounded by a rippling stream. Grateful shade is cast by large walnut trees, the deeply fissured and gnarled trunks of which rise from spreading roots which encroach on the path. Some of these trees have a girth of 18 feet and more. The houses are mostly two storied, and they have a framework of wood which is filled in with sun-dried or, in the better houses, with red kiln-baked bricks. Under the thatched roofs is an airy space with stores of grass and firewood, and sometimes silkworms. The eggs of the latter are imported from France and to a less extent from Italy, and about 30,000 ounces are distributed annually to villagers, who place them in the roofs or rooms of their houses and hatch them. The young are then fed on the leaves of the mulberry trees which are so common. The cocoons when ready are purchased by the silk factory. In this way as much as 3,200,000 lbs. may be brought in by the villagers in one year, for which the Department of Sericulture pays over Rs. 600,000 (about £40,000). This goes to about thirty-five thousand villagers, giving them on an average nearly Rs. 11/ each, which makes it quite worth their while, as this is equivalent to at least two months' wages for an ordinary Kashmiri cultivator.

Most of the houses have a front verandah to the upper story in which the people live for the greater part of the year, and at one end of which is a little kitchen with clay fireplace. The inner rooms, chiefly used in winter, are dark and almost unventilated. The ground floor is often set apart entirely for cattle and sheep. If this arrangement secures warmth for the dwellers above, it is at some sacrifice of sweetness. Every village has several granaries, small square wooden buildings, the floor of which is raised a few feet above the ground. And not far away is sure to be a village shrine (Astán) often on an eminence and usually with fine old trees in the vicinity. The Mosque is probably near by, and in its roof may be seen the wooden bier in which the dead are carried to the graveyard to be interred without a coffin. At daybreak and at sunset the voice of the *muezzin* sounds out, calling the faithful to prayer, and soon a small congregation gathers and the Imam conducts the Namáz. In some mosques the congregation chant their prayers almost in Gregorian style.

Often the sides of the houses are festooned with bright rows of red chillies or split turnips, golden maize cobs and dried apples.

In the courtyard in front of a house we see two women busily engaged in pounding the unhusked rice in a large wooden mortar with pestles 5 feet long. First one straightens herself, lifts the pestle as high as she can, and then bending suddenly brings it down with a crash. Then the other woman facing her does the same. This is perhaps one of the commonest sights in the village. On a stretch of green, there is a row of upright sticks at intervals of 2 feet. These are for weaving purposes. One of the villagers may be seen walking up and down rapidly winding from a spindle a thread of cotton in and out of these stakes. In the verandah an old woman is seated with masses of snow-white cotton-wool in front of her, from which, with the aid of a curious old wheel, she is spinning excellent thread. A peep through the window of another house shows a rough loom in which woollen blankets are woven. This is one of the staple village industries. A common arrangement is for the local shopkeeper to advance money on the promise of repayment in blankets and garden produce.

According to the Kashmiris there are six seasons in the year, each of two months. "Wandh," with a somewhat similar sound, corresponds to our English winter, or at least with the time from 15th November till 15th January. During this period and on till the end of March, the first ploughing for wheat and barley is done. Then rice, maize and the other autumn crops are threshed; and when the snow falls towards the end of December the people weave woollen blankets, and attend to their sheep and cattle. "Sont" is the period from 15th March to 1st May. This is an extremely busy time. The fields have to be ploughed and manured for rice and maize. And then these are sown. In many villages the rice is sown in nurseries, and the seedlings are planted out when they are nearly a foot high.

Broadcast sowing gives better crops but entails considerably more labour in weeding. The wheat and barley harvest begins in the valley at the end of May, and during the whole summer the harvest goes on at the various altitudes. Linseed is a little later than wheat. From July to September the peasants are busy in the fields weeding the rice, maize and cotton.

The last is a very pretty crop, with its large yellow flowers followed by snowy tufts. The real harvest of Kashmir comes on in September and October, called by the Kashmiris the season of "Hard." It is then that the rice and maize, millet, sesame, amaranth and other autumn crops are gathered in. And now the fruit trees are laden, and before long from all parts of the valley strings of ponies may be met, and lines of coolies carrying baskets of apples and pears and sacks of walnuts, most of which will find their way to Baramula and be exported from there by cart to the plains of India.

At harvest-time all round the valley, but especially near the fringe of the forest, the villagers are troubled by the depredations of bears. The fields of maize and the fruit on the trees are a great attraction. To guard their crops the people erect "machans"—little roofed platforms twelve to twenty feet above the ground. Here they sit and watch at night and blow trumpets, beat drums, old kerosene tins, or anything else which will make a noise. And at the same time they emit blood-curdling yells, or piercing whistles, all with the object of terrifying the nocturnal robbers. The combined effect of fifty or a hundred people thus engaged at night over a comparatively small area of cultivated land is somewhat suggestive of pandemonium.

Kashmir is particularly rich in fruit trees. Many of these are indigenous and found wild in the forests. The people are quite clever at grafting. The stock is cut off rather low, and into the end three or four scions are wedged and supported by clay surrounded by birch bark. Ring budding is also successfully practised. In addition to the ordinary fruit trees, currants, raspberries and gooseberries are found wild. Apricots are also common. The fruit has been all immensely improved by cultivation and the introduction of choice varieties.

The grapes are rather disappointing. In the valley, rapid night radiation in the autumn, and the heavy dew, together with the great sun heat in the day, appear to favour blight and other disease. At the mouth of the Sind valley there are some good vineyards producing delicious white and red dessert grapes.

On the east side of the Dal Lake there are about 400 acres of wine grapes, and at the distillery, under M. Peychaud's skilled supervision, wines of the Barsac and Medoc type are produced. The vintage varies much from year to year. It is said that the soil is deficient in iron and phosphates, and that the frequent difficulty in obtaining perfectly ripe grapes affects both the quality and keeping powers of the wine.

Hops grow well in Kashmir. In the summer the growth is very rapid. A market is found for them in the Murree and other breweries.

A large number of sheep are kept by peasants who live in the valley. These all have to be sent up to the hill pastures in the summer to escape the intense heat and get fresh grazing. They are entrusted to shepherds who bring them back again in the autumn and receive two per cent. of the flock if it is intact. They are also paid in rice and are allowed all the butter made from the sheep's milk.

The cows, which are numerous in the villages, are small, and they usually appear to be half starved. They seldom give more than six pints of milk a day. A cow may be bought for about twenty rupees.

In the sides of some of the houses in the villages we see a circle with a hole in the centre into which bees are seen to be crowding. These are the Kashmir hives.

They are merely earthenware cylinders, about 2 feet long, and built into the wall. The outside end of the hive has a central hole about an inch across, or sometimes a series of small holes in a circle. The inner end has an earthenware lid fitted over it and sealed on with clay. No artificial feeding is done in the summer, but in winter the bees are supplied with food. No special measures are, however, taken to protect them from the cold, and the mortality is often very great. In many villages, after a severe winter, when the temperature sometimes falls to zero Fahrenheit, more than three-quarters of the colonies will perish. Under favourable conditions strong colonies are formed. Early in May the swarms issue. One hive may give off as many as six, weighing from two to four pounds each. The villagers usually expect the swarms to settle and hive themselves in one of the numerous empty wall hives. The bees are not accustomed to English hives, and it is extremely difficult to retain them. In many cases it appears advisable to fit a strip of queen excluder zinc across the entrance to prevent the queen from leaving. Usually this can be safely removed after two or three weeks. But I have frequently lost swarms in spite of this precaution. One colony left the hive and deserted its brood two months after it had been introduced. This was, however, due to persistent attacks of bee-robbers. Where Kashmir bees are kept in wooden hives there seems to be an unusual amount of fighting and robbing. The local earthenware hives do not appear to attract outsiders. Hornets, however, are often seen attempting to get in. The wooden hives perhaps emit an odour from their joints, for they are pestered by hornets, worried by robbers, and sometimes in the spring a swarm will descend upon an already occupied hive.

The Kashmiris understand something of the management of queens. They sometimes secure a restless queen by tying a fine thread to one of her legs and pinning her to the comb. Sometimes, too, they change queens, and they cut out queen cells quite cleverly.

Two harvests may be obtained, one in June and the other

in October. The back of the hive is opened and smoke is blown in, and the combs are rapidly cut out. The bees are gentle, so comparatively few are killed. No proper care is usually taken of brood comb, and insufficient supplies are often left for the survivors. Sulphur is, however, not used.

The bees are wonderfully tame. I have often manipulated them without the use of any subduer. As in Europe, there appear to be two chief varieties—the yellow bee and a darker kind. In the yellow variety there is a fairly broad transverse stripe on the back, with four parallel pale yellow bands below. The ventral surface of the abdomen is yellow, and the thorax is covered with light brown fur. The lowest stripe is a little broader at the middle, which makes the bee look as if it had a white tail. The wings when folded reach to the lower margin of this stripe.

Wild bees appear to be yellower and to have slightly longer bodies than the domesticated varieties. I have seen them as high as 12,000 feet above sea-level. The favourite altitude for wild colonies is between 5500 and 7000 feet. It is too hot for them in the valley in the summer; but all round the hills in the mountain villages they thrive. The forests are full of wild balsams and the slopes are covered with wild sage. So great is the attraction of the mountain and forest flowers that many swarms desert the valley in the spring but return to their village hives again in September.

Both hornets and ants are troublesome enemies. When hornets threaten the hive the bees come out and form compact groups, and as the enemy approaches they lower their heads and, with a peculiar quivering movement, turn their tails with the sting exposed towards the intruder, who usually veers off. Hornets, however, sometimes carry off one or even two bees at a time. Occasionally a bee with bold spirit takes decisive action. Perhaps, like Sir Nigel Loring, she regards the hornet as a " courteous and worthy person with whom some small bickering may be had." Or possibly, Marcus Curtius like, she seeks, by sacrificing herself, to save the whole community. I have seen a bee suddenly dash out from the armed circle of defenders and pierce a formidable hornet four times her own size, inflicting a fatal wound. But all are not so courageous, for one day I placed a dead hornet on the alighting-board when the sentry had gone in for a moment. A casual bee coming out for an evening walk suddenly and unexpectedly caught sight of the orange-coloured monster, gave a most dramatic start, and then hastened back to her own quarters. Whether she spread the alarming news I know not, but almost at once a fierce and stalwart worker emerged and, single-handed, seized the unwelcome intruder and threw him off the platform. In their behaviour toward ants bees seem rather timid. Ignoring them unless they come quite near, they even then appear to chase them with some apprehension lest the ant should turn and seize them by the nose.

Large ants are the most formidable of all foes. They will sometimes raid a hive like a band of Masai warriors attacking a village. There is a large black variety half an inch long, with powerful mandibles, with which they literally cut off the bees' heads. Should an invasion of these occur, the bees will leave the hive, but not before large numbers have been massacred. Fortunately the defence is easy, as it is only necessary to stand the legs of the hive in water.

No one in Kashmir has yet succeeded in getting bees to work properly in the upper sections of a standard frame hive.

It will be interesting to see whether the introduction of English or Italian queens will result in greater industry, or whether their progeny, too, will succumb to the somewhat enervating influence of the climate and the summer and autumn droughts.

As the autumn draws on in Kashmir the days remain bright and hot, but the cold at nights becomes increasingly intense. Early in September excellent snipe-shooting is to be obtained, and large numbers of duck begin to fly over the valley. On some of the lakes wild waterfowl are very abundant. In 1906 Lord Minto and the Viceregal party shot 1500 duck in one day on the Hukra Jheel. When shooting is going on, the duck rise from the lakes and marshes in clouds and wheel round in tens of thousands, some at a great height.

After the middle of October the leaves rapidly change their colour. Poplars and mulberries become lemon-yellow, chenars a pure light red, and apples and pears orange and crimson. At this season the willows are pollarded and their saplings and leaves stored for winter fodder for the flocks. In the hedges blackberries are abundant. In the evenings at this time of the year a blue mist hangs over the valley and round the foot of the mountains, which take on exceedingly rich orange-coloured tints as the sun sets.

In the winter snow usually falls in the third week of December. After that, sometimes for six weeks, the whole country is snow-bound, clouds settle down upon the mountains and there is no sunshine. The cold then becomes very great. Occasionally the Dal Lake is frozen sufficiently to bear. I have on two occasions skated from the distillery at the south end to beyond the Nassim Bagh, 3 miles to the north-west. It is not, however, very safe, as there are warm springs.

Every morning, during the winter, thousands of jackdaws leave the city and fly in dense clouds out into the country in search of food. About five o'clock in the evening they return. In fine weather they fly high. If, however, the weather is threatening, they skim just over the tops of the houses and trees. It is interesting to watch their flight. The whole army appears to be composed of divisions. As they advance, a cloud of scouts is thrown out in front. On reaching the outskirts of the city the front battalions settle on groups of trees in such numbers that the whole tree becomes black and the branches are weighed down. When the rear divisions arrive there is much wheeling and manœuvring and evidently different clans occupy distinct trees, for which sometimes active skirmishing is carried on. When, however, the last stragglers have arrived, the whole force rises in a dark cloud and makes its way to the city, where the night is spent roosting in trees and under the eaves of houses.

The valley of Kashmir is remarkably calm. With the exception of thunderstorms in the summer and occasional gales early in March, it is extremely rare to have a windy day. The rainfall varies much from year to year. It is usually between twenty-five and thirty-five inches. The heaviest rain is ordinarily towards the end of July, corresponding to the full development of the monsoon in North India, and it is then that there is great danger of floods.

One of the commonest of Kashmir birds in the villages is the white-cheeked bulbul. These have a graceful feather crest curving forwards and nearly 2 inches long. They are quite domesticated and often come indoors, perching on tables and chairs or even on the edge of a tea-cup, the sugar at the bottom of which has special attractions for them. With a little trouble they can be taught to catch crumbs thrown in the air, and they will perch on the back of one's hand. Swallows are exceedingly common. They usually arrive in March and build their nests in April and May.

Small game is not nearly so common in Kashmir as might be expected. There are no hares nor wild rabbits in the valley. On the hills the chikor partridge is common. It belongs to the genus of rock or sand partridges, and is found usually just above the line of cultivation among the rocks. Coveys are often seen in the fields at harvest-time, and they are met with up to an altitude of 9000 feet. The monal pheasant is the most handsome of all Kashmir birds. The cock is magnificent, with rich peacock-blue plumage with golden-red sheen. These pheasants are not very common. They live chiefly at the upper margins of the forests.

The valley is infested with rats. In the summer they live in the fields and farmyards. In the winter they crowd into the houses and do immense mischief. They would be still more numerous were it not for the large number of half-wild cats which take up their abode in the roofs and basements of the houses and do valuable service. It is an interesting fact that when Kashmir was attacked by plague there was no evidence of any rat infection.

As we walk through the village we notice the little shop, the tawny-yellow or black dogs stealthily walking about, the flocks of ducks busy gobbling in the stream and the little bathing-houses close by.

Ploughing is done with small bullocks and the ploughs are small, for deep furrows are unnecessary. Rice cultivation is the great interest of most of the inhabitants of the valley. It speaks well for the fertility of Kashmir that although there is only one annual rice crop, in good years excellent rice may be bought at a halfpenny per pound.

It is in the villages that we see the real Kashmir life. The language, dress, complexion, manners and customs of the people here are quite distinct from those of any other country. Probably few people have undergone less change in the march of the centuries than this nation, in its isolated valley, separated by gigantic mountain ranges from all the countries around and, until the last quarter of a century, connected with India only by a rough bridle track more than a hundred miles long.

CHAPTER IX

MEDICAL MISSION CAMP WORK

On the March—Methods of Work—Worship of Sacred Places—The Pirs—The Great Flood—Relief Work.

Go with the spiritual life, the higher volition and action,
With the great girdle of God, go and encompass the earth!—
Not for the gain of the gold, for the getting, the hoarding, the having,
But for the joy of the deed;—but for the Duty to do!

CLOUGH.

To come into really close contact with the people it is necessary to go and live among them. This can be done by going into camp. Firstly we gather together a good supply of medicines. These and our surgical instruments, dressings, tents, bedding, clothes, etc., are packed up into separate bundles, altogether about ten in number. Next day they are all put on board one of the flat-bottomed river-boats. We embark, with a dispenser and a surgical assistant, and quietly drift down the stream. Presently night comes, but our boat continues its course, one or two strokes of the paddle at the back, every now and then, keeping the bows straight. Early the next morning we come to an immense stretch of water, the Wular Lake. The boatmen always cross this with great trepidation, as it is exposed to severe storms which sometimes come on suddenly and are occasionally destructive to life. Under favourable circumstances we reach the other side by midday. The next step is to obtain porters to carry our baggage over the mountain-passes. The following morning we make an early start and begin climbing up steep grassy slopes. Then the path enters a great pine forest. As we approach the summit of the pass, looking back, we obtain a magnificent view of the Wular Lake, glittering in the sunshine, 3000 feet below, with the Vale of Kashmir extending away into the dim distance beyond.

Crossing the ridge, we descend gradually through dense fir forest until the trees begin to get thinner and more scattered.

Kashmir has its backwoods—stretches of sloping hillsides, partly under cultivation, with green patches of Indian corn rudely fenced in by primitive hedges of broken tree trunks. Here and there are groups of blackened tree trunks. Close by is the margin of the great forest, home of the bear and leopard. Troops of monkeys may be seen, swinging from tree to tree, or grouped in grassy glades, munching wild apples, green walnuts, or any other forest fruits upon which they can put their paws. Sometimes they are so near that you are tempted to chase them. If you do so you will find that instead of running off along the ground where they could easily outdistance you, they will almost at once take to some high tree, perhaps a fir, up which they will run till they reach the top branches, where they sit and calmly survey you to see what you intend to do next. The settlers who live in the flat, earthen-roofed log huts, which are scattered about in the newly-reclaimed fields, have to reckon with these predatory bands, which systematically rob their crops.

It was in such a district as this that I took up my quarters for a short time in the month of May. The hut in which I was staying is on the very border of the forest. Behind lay a fringe of blue pines, with cedars and spruce trees, gradually becoming more and more dense. In front was the dark brown of the rich newly turned-up soil; a little further away the gleam of flooded rice-fields; and here and there a grove of walnut trees, from among which peep out the roofs and walls of dark brown log huts.

The news soon spreads that the doctor has arrived. And early in the morning little groups of expectant patients may be seen sitting beneath the pine trees. Their numbers are continually being added to, until at last there may be as many as a hundred and fifty or two hundred people. Herdsmen there are, and numbers of ordinary Kashmiri peasants; a sprinkling of Punjabis, who have come as emigrants; two or three Hindus, distinguishable by the vertical reddish-yellow mark on their foreheads; and shyly holding aloof there are also groups of women, some clad in dirty grey gowns which were once white, and others, the wives and daughters of Gujars, dressed in dark blue.

Our stock of medicines and instruments is arranged on a table and all the scattered clumps of people are gathered together in a semicircle facing the doctor, who briefly explains to them all his object in visiting the district; that he has come to endeavour to help those who are sick; that he has come from the well-known hospital at Drogjun, Srinagar. Here, perhaps, one or two of those present say that they have been there, and were with us for some time, and were kindly treated and got well. Resuming, the doctor goes on to say that he has also come to tell them all the Good News of the Gospel of Christ. Here some one present interrupts and is understood to say that this was what he heard when he was in the hospital, and that it was good doctrine. The doctor then reads some short passage to the assembled crowd, which is being constantly augmented by fresh arrivals, and in simple phrases in their own Kashmiri language tells them the old story of the sinfulness of man, the love of God and its manifestation in our Saviour Christ. The audience listens with marked attention, and as the doctor closes with the words that the work which is done at the hospital at Drogjun and which is also going to be done in their midst is the work of Christ, because it is at His command, in His name, by His servants and for His honour, there is a murmur of assent. After a short prayer for the blessing of God upon the work and the people, the medical part of the work is begun and goes on till all present have been seen.

Their ailments are very various. Some have old-standing indigestion or chronic coughs. Others are suffering from ophthalmia or from various parasitic diseases. The latter are largely propagated by infected drinking-water. And young children are specially liable to suffer. In most Kashmiri villages the juvenile population, instead of being strong, well, and of a healthy colour, is pale and unwholesome looking. Skin diseases, too, largely due to dirt, abound. A good many surgical cases are usually brought to us. And from a professional standpoint these are the most satisfactory of all, as we can usually either put them right at once, or give them a note of admission to the central hospital.

The work in some of its aspects, although arduous, is not without its touch of humour. In one part of the arena a line of children will be seen waiting for their dose of santonin and castor oil, which is administered in such a way as to remind one of the ministrations at Dotheboys Hall. Sitting under a tree may be seen an enthusiastic patient, carefully scraping with his forefinger the remains of castor oil from a red earthenware cup and consuming it with apparent relish. Public interest reaches a high pitch when an operation is to be done, and it is impossible to exclude unprofessional spectators. Perhaps some small tumour is removed, or a series of cases of in-turned eyelashes is operated upon, teeth are extracted, or small abscesses lanced. I often wonder whether our antiseptic precautions are not regarded as some kind of special ritual. If chloroform has to be administered the interest reaches its high-water mark, and a hush falls upon the onlookers. Next day the crowd is larger than ever, and if many days are spent at one centre the numbers are apt to become so great as to be almost unmanageable.

The importance and value of periodic tours in the outlying districts of Kashmir are obvious. Not only do these bring us into touch with remote villages, and enable us to attend to those who may require skilled treatment, but they also quicken the flow of patients from the villages to the hospital, where treatment can be carried out under the most favourable conditions, and where in the wards there is daily Christian instruction.

It is easy enough for those who live near the river to come in to the hospital, even if their homes are distant. But there are many remote mountain valleys which are difficult of access. A mountain pass more than 2000 feet high is a serious obstacle for any one who is blind, lame or otherwise disabled. Hence the recurring visits of the medical missionary are hailed with delight.

And year by year Christian teaching and the healing art have thus been carried to all parts of Kashmir. "In the Wazir Garden at Islamabad, under the chenar groves at Pampoor, by the broad placid river at Sopur, in the visitors' bungalow at Baramula, the busy portal of 'the Happy Valley,' in the stately gardens at Vernag and Achibal, by the sacred tank at Báwan, below the great mosque at Eish-makám, among the walnut trees and orchards of sequestered mountain villages, have the message of Divine love and the ministry of healing been brought to the sinful and the sick."

In Kashmir there is very little fanaticism. In some respects the toleration is surprising. The friendly relations existing between Mohammedans and Hindus are remarkable, and partly to be explained by the fact that many Hindu customs have survived, even among Mohammedans.

At the present time the Mohammedans greatly outnumber the Hindus in Kashmir, forming 93 per cent. of the total population. Forcibly converted from Hinduism in the fourteenth century, they still retain some indications of their original faith. The most striking of these is their affection for sacred places. Thus both religions have this important feature in common. For the Hindus also resort to springs, tanks and lakes. "Although great Pan be dead in Greece, the twilight of the gods is not yet in Kashmir. Every grove has its familiar deity; every clear spring or rushing torrent its water-nymph." Not a few Mohammedan shrines have been placed on the sites of former Hindu sacred springs, and the worship has been continuous, although changed in form.

A large number of villages have each their own shrine, usually the grave of some Mohammedan saint of bygone days.

Often one tank will have a Hindu "Astán" on one side and a Mohammedan "Ziarat" on the other. Recently, when on tour, I pitched my tent on a peninsula, in the middle of a tank, and the droning sound of a Hindu chanting his Shasters on one side and of a Mohammedan Darwesh reciting the Koran on the other side, seldom ceased.

In this respect the worship of Hindus and Mohammedans is similar. Indeed an easy transition seems to have occurred, when the Hindus embraced Islam, under Mohammedan pressure, and their devotion was transferred from the spring to the tomb. The oldest Mohammedan shrines now existing may be traced back to about the fourteenth century. Devotion to, reverence for, and implicit trust in the village shrine play a much larger part in the religious life of the average Kashmiri Mohammedan than any special regard for the Koran or its teaching. And although the name of Mohammed is reverenced by the people they know little about him. It is the shrine which protects from disease and disaster, and to it they look for aid in any enterprise or in times of stress. Gifts are brought to it by the villagers—fowls, rice, ghee and sometimes money. The custodians of the tombs are usually descendants of the "holy" man interred therein. They are called Pirs or Pirzádas, and wield considerable influence. They can usually read, and a common arrangement is for them to take turns in conducting the worship of the village mosque. Besides receiving the offerings of the faithful, they eke out a rather precarious livelihood by making and selling charms. These consist of a short verse of the Koran, or even an undecipherable scribble on a scrap of Kashmir paper, folded up and stitched in a little piece of cloth or leather perhaps two inches long and one and a half broad. This is tied round the neck of the applicant, or round one of his arms. If there is disease of the foot or leg the amulet may be found attached to the ankle or knee. In cases of illness the Pirzádas are usually called in and they recite prayers and issue fresh charms. The common people have great faith in these Pirs. One of the villagers, referring to the plague, which had not invaded the isolated mountain district in which his village was situated, said to me, " It has not come here, sir, the Pirs here have mighty powers."

Sometimes when we are camped in a village, the Pirs shun us. At others they are friendly, and come and listen to the preaching, and are willing to accept and even pay for little books. Occasionally they raise objections to the teaching, or ask questions which are not always relevant. In talking to them, one of the most useful arguments is the sinlessness of Our Lord. For what is required is something to show them that Christ is not as they claim, only one of a select number of great prophets, who were equal and are all mediators.

The Great Flood

" As on my return from a tour to Kishtiwar, on a cloudless June morning, I looked from a snowy pass westward for 100 miles across the great basin of the Kashmir valley, with its ripening wheat and young green maize, and the glitter of its streams and the soft blue haze of its distant towns, I little dreamt that in a few days there would be the highest flood recorded for many generations.

" Even before the heavy rain, the Wular Lake was already at its flood level, from the melting of the exceptional snows of last winter. Then came two heavy downpours, with but three days' interval. In the side valleys the bridges were swept away, and as the clouds cleared, we learnt by the telegraph that the river had risen 30 feet at the head of the valley, Islamabad. Steadily the water rose, overlapping the lofty embankments which protect the towns and cultivated areas. With ample warning the people fled from all the lower ground, carrying their little household effects. It was beautiful, but cruel; those ever-widening, ever-rising stretches of rippling, gleaming water, then the crash of the cataract and of falling houses, as the flood broke through or lapped over an embankment and swept down in resistless power, involving gardens and palings and outhouses in one common ruin. There was much to be done in the way of salvage at the English Church, at the library which fell, crushing thousands of volumes into the muddy water, and in other places. And it was a strange sight to be rowing about the Munshi Bagh in which we live, trying to avoid the masses of wreckage swept along by the swift current, and steer one's way among the upper branches of fruit trees, or past the half-submerged roofs of huts.

"The hospital, so splendidly situated on the western spur of the Takht Hill, was at once the refuge for many, and every possible part of it was occupied to overflowing, while the surrounding slopes were covered with refuge camps, and the road blocked with ekkas and carriages. At the foot of the hill house-boats and barges were moored, and rafts of timber were floating about. The scene was one of picturesque beauty, for the weather was brilliant. Among the hospital inmates were all sorts and conditions of men, Europeans, Parsees, Sikhs, Kashmiri officials and military officers as well as the usual variety of patients. For the first few days we must have numbered over 200 persons. There was almost a water famine, for the water pipes had been carried away and provisions were very scarce. We were soon active in relief work, for hundreds were homeless, and some destitute. A wealthy and philanthropic Parsee, Mr Dhanjibhoy, C.I.E., generously bought large quantities of grain in the Punjab and sent it up for us to sell at a low price; so a grain shop was opened at the hospital, of which Mr Knowles took the charge, and this rice or flour was sold below cost price to those whose houses had been destroyed. In addition to the work thus done by the Mission, there was another larger relief fund. The Kashmir State also gave a large amount of wood for the purpose of rebuilding. By invitation of the Resident, I took charge of an area of about 200 square miles of flooded district between the city and the Wular Lake. Much of my work had to be done by boat, as the water was still very high, and some of the villages surrounded by marshes had to be reached partly by wading. In the course of a month I visited about 100 villages, distributing Rs. 4000 of the State Relief Fund, issuing orders on the Forest Department for timber, and also orders for water-chestnuts, of which a large crop soon became available. Later on I was joined by Pandit Radha Kishen, formerly Chief Justice, and by Colonel G. Young, C.B. As the news of this relief spread, villagers, who had deserted their ruined homes and fled to the hills, or gone for work to the towns, began to return and collect materials and rebuild some kind of shelter from the weather. We found intense poverty in the lower villages where people were eking out an existence on herbs and the stalks of water-lilies. In one village but three families out of twenty had any kind of grain. Fortunately at that time the flocks were all on the mountains, and so were safe out of harm's way. There is much recuperative power in Kashmir villages, and with the help of grants of wood most were rebuilt before the winter.

"In my work I received considerable help from the higher State officials, and on one occasion, having run out of money, I bicycled up to the city and called on the Private Secretary to the Maharajah, and His Highness gave me Rs. 500 from his private purse to go on with. Mr Knowles and Mr Tyndale-Biscoe were doing similar work in and around the city, and we were glad to be in a position to help relieve such a catastrophe.

"The Medical Missionary needs to give a wide and liberal interpretation of his marching orders. Sanitation claims a place in the functions of the physician in all lands, not least amid the filth of the Orient." [1]

[1] A. Neve, *Mission Hospital Reports.*

CHAPTER X

A GLIMPSE OF KASHMIRI TIBET

The Sind Valley—A Delayed Post—The Zoji Pass—Dras and the Dards—Kargyl—The Battle of Pashkyum Valley—Moulbe Sculpture—Lámoyóro Monastery—A Weird Orchestra—Chunrezig—The Bon Chos—Assassination of Langdarma—A Ladákhi Village.

IT was on a beautiful day towards the end of May that I started on a journey to Leh. This town is the capital of Ladákh, a barren but very picturesque and interesting country in the midst of the Himalaya mountains between Kashmir and Chinese Tibet.

Turning our backs on the little European settlement at Srinagar, on the stately but sluggish river Jhelum, and leaving behind us the great line of glistening peaks which bound the valley of Kashmir on the south, separating it from the plains of India by a mountain barrier 150 miles wide, we rode out to Kangan, the first large village in the Sind valley, on the great high-road to Ladákh, Tibet and China. At Kangan the valley is about a mile across. The Sind River is a deep and rushing stream, fed by melting snows in the regions to which we are going. The road wends its way up this valley, sometimes close to the river, at others climbing over spurs or traversing patches of gloomy forest, again emerging and like an English country lane, bounded by rough hedgerows, rich with honeysuckle, jessamine and wild roses. Every few miles we pass a village nestling in walnut and mulberry trees; the fruit of the latter, which is ripe, is eagerly consumed by the juvenile population, which grows visibly fatter in the mulberry season. Horses, cows, sheep, goats and even dogs may be seen greedily devouring the fruit as it lies on the ground. At night, too, bears, attracted by the sweet juicy berries, sometimes come down and climb the trees. The next part of the route has an alpine beauty and passes through upland meadows brilliant with flowers—ragwort, larkspur, balsams, columbines and anemones, with a background of fir forest. This in its turn presents a dark serrated edge against the atmospheric mauve, from which rise snowy peaks and slopes like burnished silver.

Not long ago Rahmana, a postal runner, was carrying his mail-bag along this road. He had it slung over his back in a blanket. Suddenly he felt a violent blow from behind which knocked him over. On turning round he saw a large black bear standing over him. Shouting for help, he caught hold of his post-bag, which the bear was proceeding to examine, and tried to run away; but this unfortunately directed the foe's attention to him, and the bear, sitting up in its characteristic posture for attack, struck him a violent blow in the face with its right paw. Rahmana fell down again and would very likely have ended his days there and then, if some villagers, hearing his shouts, had not rushed up. The bear, seeing their numbers, judged that discretion was the better part of valour and fled. Rahmana was carried on a bedstead 20 miles to the Mission Hospital. I met him at Kangan some months afterwards when he had quite recovered, although he was sadly scarred and disfigured. "Thrice," he said, "during the first night at the hospital the night nurse came to see whether I was still breathing and thinking I might be dead, I was so weak." He spent several weeks with us and was most grateful. The Christian instruction which he had received from day to day had evidently impressed him, and he will, I know, give us a warm welcome whenever we visit his village.

Leaving Kangan, we passed the place where the day

before, the road being bad, a pack-pony belonging to Major D——, a sportsman, had fallen into the river and been swept away. The whole of that pony's baggage was lost, including rifles and money. As we went on, the valley became narrower and the sides steeper. Clouds had been gathering, and suddenly a terrific storm came on, the thunder rolling round and reverberating among the cliffs and mountains. The rain continued, and we were soon thoroughly drenched and our baggage (on pack-ponies) well soaked. The water was running off the ground in sheets and night was coming on. Pitching tents was out of the question, so we took shelter in a house in the village of Revil. The owner, who was sitting in a kind of verandah, swept it out for us and here we established ourselves.

The next day being Sunday, we made a halt, and soon found that sick people were beginning to arrive. So we unpacked our medicine boxes and soon all the village had gathered round. Amongst others was a former hospital patient, who, like Rahmana, had been attacked and severely mauled by a bear. He brought a present of honey and then proceeded in Oriental fashion to descant to the assembled crowd on the excellences of the Mission Hospital and how well he was treated there.

Great wreaths of white cloud were drifting along the hillsides and the fresh snow was quite near us. But the next day, in spite of rain, we pushed on.

A few miles further up the geological formation is interesting and characteristic. From just below Gagangair in the S.W. in ascending order, as we march up the gorge N.E. to Sonamarg, we notice schistose slates, quartzite, lower carboniferous (*syringothyris*) limestone, agglomeratic slate, with traces of fenestella beds and Punjal trap. Finally, at Sonamarg, above all, are permo-carboniferous layers and muschelkalk. In the latter, fossil *Ptychites* have been found by Stolkza and by Middlemiss. The latter points

23. THE ZOJI LÁ PASS.

out that the sections of the Lidar valley show exactly the same sequence.

The scenery was now very fine. The valley became narrower and narrower until at last it formed a great rift or chasm, with the river foaming at the bottom. Our road, which was several hundred feet above it, was carefully built on the steep hillside. Opposite it were beetling cliffs nearly a mile high, with here and there between them patches of gloomy pine forest. Two more days brought us to the foot of the Zoji Pass, the boundary between fertile Kashmir, with its flowery meadows and dense forests and the barren rainless upland valleys of Dras and Ladákh (Plate 23).

The top of the Zoji La Pass is about 11,200 feet above sea-level, and although easy in the summer and autumn, when the path ascends through graceful birch woods and over green slopes studded with pink primulas or brilliant red potentillas, it is difficult to cross in the winter or spring on account of the deep snow. Rising at 3.30 a.m., we had not gone far before our difficulties commenced. The snow was too slippery for laden ponies, and in places snow bridges had broken away. We were obliged to unload, and, with the aid of some hardy mountaineers, carried our baggage over the difficult and dangerous places. Presently the snow seemed harder and we again loaded the ponies, but even then, ever and anon, one would fall through up to his girths. After seven hours' hard work we reached a shelter hut. The worst of the pass was now over. Some months later a Moravian missionary, Mr Francke, very nearly lost his life trying to cross too early in March. He was overwhelmed by a heavy snowstorm, lost his way, fell into a drift and gave himself up as lost, when providentially he saw in the distance the dim forms of two postal runners, and following in their track he extricated himself.

In the shelter house we found a solitary traveller—strange to say, a former hospital patient on his way home—

an old man very feeble and with a bad cough. He had been unable to proceed and might have died but for our arrival. Giving him food, we put him on a pony and carried him safely on his journey for some days, till we reached a large village. On the way we were caught in a sharp snowstorm and passed the skeleton of some poor traveller who had perished by the way.

After two days we reached Dras. This is a small village in a wide open valley 10,000 feet above sea-level. Amid grassy slopes and patches of cultivation there are detached groups of flat-topped houses, and for such a remote place there is a fair population.

Dras is one of the districts where there are descendants of the Dard invaders who entered Western Tibet from the north-west; but having become Mohammedans, these have lost many of their distinctive features. On the other side of Kargyl, to the north-east, there are, however, still some genuine Dards, who have kept up old customs, including a special festival every two or three years, when they sing Dard songs. Both here and at Dras the Dard language is spoken. It is strange that there are so few of these Dard colonists left. Mr Francke gives the following story which he has heard of their fall. "The Dards were besieged in their castle (probably by Tibetans), and when their supplies of food and water came to an end, they resolved to die together. So they all assembled in the central hall of the castle and the oldest man pushed away the stone on which stood the central pillar supporting the roof and the falling roof buried them all." The Dards were fond of adorning rocks with outline drawings of animals. The ibex is the favourite, but mounted huntsmen and even tigers are occasionally represented. And various symbols and stone images show that they were Buddhists.

At Dras more than seventy patients came to me in one day. One of the bystanders interpreted for me from Kashmiri to Tibetan. The head magistrate of the district happened to be there and sat by my side. He also accepted a copy of the Gospels in Persian.

Just beyond Dras, on the plateau, there are some interesting stone images by the wayside. One of these bears an inscription in Kashmiri Sharáda characters, which was partly deciphered by Cunningham, who made out amongst others the word "Matreiyan." In all probability these are Buddhist images, dating back to the emigration from Kashmir.

The news of our coming now preceded us, and, as we marched on, often we would find a little group of patients and their friends waiting by the roadside to interview us. Here and there a former patient would appear. One old man, for instance, had received his sight after an operation for cataract. Further on we met a cripple being carried in a basket *en route* for the Mission Hospital, which was now ten days' journey away. Sometimes a blanket was spread on the ground for us to sit on and dishes of dried apricots and their kernels and currants were brought out. The people are pleasant-mannered but very dirty. In some districts their lives are hard, owing to the difficulty in raising crops in the desert. Nothing can be done without irrigation. Wherever a stream comes down from the snow-clad heights, there is a fan-shaped area of cultivation, and little channels are cut along the hillside as far as the water can be carried. In some villages there are three or four lines of small irrigation canals one above the other. Occasionally they may be seen hundreds of feet above the road. These channels were many of them perhaps constructed in the first instance by the Dards.

The sands of some of the rivers, the banks of which we were now marching along, contain a fair amount of gold. In some places the people do gold-washing, but their methods are primitive and they make little more than the daily wages of an ordinary labourer. Here and there one finds evident traces of old workings. There are, for instance, remains of gold-diggings near Channegund, 7 miles before we come to Kargyl.

The next day we reached Kargyl, which is a large village and marks the border where we pass into Ladákh. In the villages on the Kashmir side there are some Hindus and Sikhs, but most of the people are Mussulmans, and Mohammedanism is now spreading chiefly by intermarriage with Tibetan women. In Kargyl both polygamy and polyandry exist side by side.

In Tibet polyandry is the custom. This has been defended, even by British officials, on the ground that the country is too poor to support a population married in the ordinary manner. The fallacy of this would be less obvious if the unmarried women of Tibet remained virgins, which is not the case. Moreover, the practice of polygamy, which in the case of Tibetan Mohammedans is becoming more frequent, has shown no signs of producing a population too large for the districts where it is in vogue. Most of the people in Kargyl understand Tibetan only, but there are very few Buddhists. After Kargyl the population is Buddhist and you feel that you are in a strange country.

Here and there on the hill-tops or by the wayside are to be seen the simple square altars known as lathos, which date back to before the introduction of Buddhism, but upon which people still place flowers and hang strips of rag as an offering to " the Unknown God."

On leaving Kargyl we crossed the Suru River which carries down masses of dark-coloured silt, and climbing up 200 feet we crossed a bare and arid plateau surrounded on every side by high but barren peaks. After 7 miles we descended to a stream and found vegetation again—willow-trees, poplars, barley and wild roses.

This is known as the Pashkyum valley, and was the scene of a great battle in the autumn of 1834, when the Dogras, under Zoráwar, invaded Ladákh. The Ladákhi leader fell early in the day and his army at once fled in the direction of Moulbé and Shergol, destroying the bridge to prevent pursuit. The Dogras, however, crossed the river on inflated skins, inflicted great slaughter and also captured some hundreds of the fugitives who were neither so well armed as themselves nor possessed of discipline.

Winter came on and the Ladákhis had their chance, but their leaders were absolutely incompetent. Mustering an army of about 15,000, they again marched down to attack the Dogras near Langkartse, between Kargyl and Suru. But on the approach of the Dogras they again fled, losing 400 of their number who fell through a snow bridge and were drowned and 200 who were made prisoners, including their general. The Ladákhis then retreated to Moulbé. The Dogras followed them up and the Ladákhi army retired to Leh. All the chief towns along the route now hastened to make their submission and sent large presents to Zoráwar. In this way Lámoyóro, Saspool and Alchi escaped being sacked. The Ladákhi king, having capitulated, Zoráwar entered Leh and received a substantial indemnity of 50,000 rupees and he also arranged for an annual tribute of Rs. 20,000.

Meanwhile a Dogra fort at Suru had been attacked by the chief of Sod, who captured it and killed the garrison. Zoráwar, who heard of this when at Lámoyóro, at once marched to Suru, put the small Ladákhi garrison to the sword, and, by offering 50 rupees per head on all who had joined the chief of Sod's force, 200 were surrendered to him. These he beheaded.

Leaving Pashkyum behind us, we plunged into a narrow rocky valley, devoid of all verdure except here and there where a little rivulet trickling down the hillside supplies sufficient water for trees and grass to grow. These spots were welcome oases in the desert. In some places the mountains were wonderfully tinted—red, yellow and violet, due to the colour of the soil.

After we had marched about 20 miles from Kargyl, emerging from a long and narrow ravine, we entered a wider valley and saw opposite to us, on the side of the hill at Sheogol, the first monastery, a small group of square white buildings with flat roofs, the edges of which were painted dark red, perched on a cliff of conglomerate.

A little farther on we caught sight of the Moulbé Lámaserai, right on top of a pointed hill 300 feet high, standing out in the valley. Just beyond Moulbé there is an immense block of rock by the roadside with beautifully sculptured on one face of it an image of Buddha 40 feet high. This Matreiya was probably carved by order of one of the local chiefs in the time of their independence (Plate 24).

At Moulbé there is also an inscription of King Lde's abolishing living sacrifices. This was not, however, obeyed, and the people continued to sacrifice goats before the pre-Buddhist altars, tearing the heart out of the living animal.

During the next two days, two lofty mountain passes had to be crossed, one of them 14,000 feet high. There was no snow here, but the height made us feel rather short of breath, especially when the wind was blowing. Descending from this, we soon came in sight of the great Buddhist monastery of Lámoyóro (Plate 25). This is a remarkable place. The high conglomerate cliffs are crowned by an immense number of buildings. Time fails to tell of all the wonders we saw—the steep stairs and ladders, the tunnel-like passages, giddy precipices, curious little cells and fierce Tibetan mastiffs, the rows of prayer cylinders, the painted stones, and strangest of all the large wall frescoes of hideous demons, and the interior of the temples. We went into two of these. The first was a room about 30 feet square and lofty, all the light, coming from little windows round the top. On the floor were rows of flat legless benches for the Lámas (as the Buddhist priests are called in Ladákh). Round the walls were

24. COLOSSAL BUDDHA AT MOULBÉ.

25. LÁMOYORO MONASTERY.

shelves and pigeon-holes full of books, manuscripts and vestments, and here also were massive copper and brass bowls, jugs, urns, basins, and the drums, cymbals, clarionets and shawms—these last 14 feet long—used by the monastery band. The walls and wooden pillars of the temple are hung with tapestry, ancient silk banners and pictures. Facing the door at the end of the room there is an altar or raised platform with rows of images of Buddhist saints. These vary in height from four inches to eight feet, and are of metal or gilded or painted clay (Plate 33). In this chamber the monks gather daily at stated times. Their ritual is interesting and impressive. Sitting in two lines facing each other, they softly chant their prayers to the rhythmical accompaniment of several drums, which are lightly tapped. At the end of a verse or paragraph a blast of trumpets, shawms and clarionets and a crash of cymbals and drums startles the visitor. The musical effect is quite unique. The sounds cease as suddenly as they began, and then one thin nasal-toned voice goes on softly chanting, to be joined shortly by the whole choir, accompanied by the drums as before (Plate 27). In some of their observances there are certain resemblances to Roman ritual. Often in reading or chanting, each monk will take different pages of the same book and read it simultaneously so as to finish the book at one sitting. Everything had a Chinese look. The banners and several of the images, with their almond-shaped eyes and gaudy colours, were identical with those which I have seen in China. So also were the rows of brass cups and little lamps and the large bowl of butter with an ever-burning wick. Most of the things in the temple had come from Lhassa, the home or Lámaism.

On special occasions the Lámas wear red cloth helmets and waistcoats of rich embroidery over their brick-red toga-like robes. In the second temple at Lámoyóro the walls are covered with frescoes illustrating Buddhist doctrine, the triumph of Buddha over his enemies and the tortures of the

Buddhist hell, and there is a large image of Chunrézig 10 feet high with numerous arms, and hands each containing an open eye.

The Dulai Láma professes to be an incarnation of Chunrézig or Avalokita. The meaning of the name is "He who looks down." This is a purely mythological creation and is met with in various forms in different parts of Tibet. The Lámoyóro image is of the colossal eleven-headed, thousand-handed form. In one of the hands is a bow and arrow for the defence of its votaries. The faces in front are supposed to wear an aspect of benevolence, while those on the left indicate anger at the sins of men. Waddell points out that the earliest images of Avalokita clearly show that the figure was modelled on the pattern of Brahma, the Hindu Creator, and that Brahma's insignia, the lotus, rosary, vase and book, may often be seen in the representations of Avalokita. Our illustration shows a rosary and vase, and in one of the right hands is a jewel (Plate 26).

In niches in the walls of the passages of the Lámoyóro monastery, and especially near the chief gateways, are the prayer cylinders, from one and a half to two feet high, each revolving on a pivot. These boxes either have a prayer painted on them outside or an opening into which a prayer sheet can be thrust. The monks as they pass set them in motion. A certain number are kept constantly revolving by water power or wind—a curiously mechanical and degraded idea of prayer. The sacred text, "Om máne padme hon," is also stamped on pieces of paper or white and yellow cotton cloth and hung up on poles. The Lámoyóro monastery is one of the most important in Ladákh and is said to have been originally a Bonpo Lámaserai. In olden times the religion of the Tibetans was the so-called Bon Chos. When Buddhism was introduced the original Tibetan religion underwent certain modifications. Monasteries were founded and the names of various spirits were tabulated. According to Francke, the main features of this religion were the follow-

26. IMAGE OF CHUNRÉZIG.

(Interior of temple at Lámoyúro.)

ing: "The world consists of three great realms, the land of the gods, or heaven, which is of white colour; the land of men, or the earth, of red colour; and the land of the water spirits or lower world, of blue colour. There is a king reigning in heaven as well as in the under world, but the greatest power on the earth is the earth mother. There is a huge tree, the tree of the world, growing through all the three realms. It has its roots in the under world and its highest branches in heaven. The king of heaven is asked to send one of his sons as king to the earth, and around the story of the mission of the youngest son of the king of heaven to the earth, the national epic of Tibet in general, and Western Tibet in particular, has grown up."

In 900 A.D. the leader of the Bon Chos was Langdarma. He carried on a campaign against Buddhism, with bitter irony, compelling many of the monks to become hunters or even butchers and beheading those who would not submit. "But when Langdarma imagined that he had succeeded in annihilating Buddhism, the snake which he thought he had crushed bit him. A Buddhist hermit put on a robe, black on the outside and white inside, because only black clothing (the colour of the Bon Chos) was allowed to be worn in those days. But underneath his coat he kept a bow and arrow in readiness. He approached the king as if he were a suppliant, and threw himself down upon the floor. When Langdarma walked up to him, he suddenly rose and shot the king through the heart. Then in order not to be recognized by those who had seen him enter in black, he put on his dress with the white outside and escaped" (Francke).

Even to this day the Ladákhi ex-kings wear their hair in the same fashion as Langdarma did. A great grandson of Langdarma, whose name was Nyima Gon, conquered the whole of Western Tibet, although to begin with he had only 300 horsemen.

At the foot of the cliffs below the Lámoyóro Monastery is the village, a group of flat-topped houses made of sun-dried bricks and nearly every one of which flies on the roof one or more prayer flags. Many of the people, too, carry prayer wheels, each consisting of a small copper cylinder 4 inches high, with a little weight and chain on one side by which it is kept constantly revolving on a wooden handle.

The approach to Lámoyóro, like that to all Lámaserais, is marked by stone walls paved with thousands of stones with the mystic formula carved on them. These walls, which are from ten to fifteen feet broad and about five feet in height, are sometimes two or three hundred yards long, and often at both ends there are chortens or rows of them.

Day after day our route lies along valleys through bare mountains, a mixture of rocky crag and sandy waste, broken only at intervals of six or eight miles by an occasional fan-shaped oasis, watered by some snow-fed stream, and assiduously cultivated by a scanty population.

A Ladákhi village is quite characteristic and very picturesque. After a long and hot march on a sandy path, with rocky cliffs towering above and a great river foaming below; after threading one's way through innumerable boulders with dark red polished surfaces and occasional carved inscriptions, all lying under a blazing sun, the atmosphere quivering with heat—the temperature in the sun perhaps 140° F.—we see in the distance a green patch of cultivation. As we approach we find terraced fields of barley and buckwheat supported by stone walls. Here and there are bushes of wild roses with profuse and brilliant red blossom. Little runlets of crystal water cross the path, and there are lines of poplars and willows with, nestling among them, flat-topped houses with bunches of prayer flags. By the side of the road are long lines of broad and solid wall, paved with smooth flat stones, each bearing the sacred text, "Om máne padme hon," "O God the jewel in the lotus. Amen." The Buddhist monuments (chortens) are a conspicuous feature of the

landscape, being pure white or earth-coloured with patches of red paint. They are usually dome-shaped, resting on a solid square foundation and with a red-coloured spire. They vary in height from twenty to sixty feet. The people are clad in long coats of a grey woollen material, with broad girdles of blue or red and caps of various colours, red, blue, green, or even of black velvet with red lining. They have high cheek-bones and wear their hair in long queues which make their backs greasy and black. The women have head-dresses of red cloth, covering also the neck and back and closely studded with turquoises and brooches. On either side these are balanced by large ear-flaps of black lamb's-wool. The poorer women wear long and thick black coats and trousers. Those who are less poor have richly-coloured stuff or silk skirts. They also wear elaborate necklaces of silver and red coral, and a large white section of some marine shell, like a cuff, on each wrist. Over all, long cloaks of goatskin are worn. The monks, too, are always in evidence, with their shaven heads, receding foreheads, voluminous red robes and bare arms.

Perhaps on top of a neighbouring cliff is a monastery, a small replica of Lámoyóro, a picturesque group of white buildings with verandahs and rows of small windows, the whole surmounted by a parapet decorated with tufts of yaks' tails on poles. In such a monastery there are usually two temples. One of these contains numerous small images of incarnations and founders, and is provided with shelves for manuscripts, brass vessels and musical instruments used in worship. In the other temple there is usually a colossal image of Buddha or Chunrézig and the walls are covered with paintings representing victories of Buddha and the destruction of his enemies. Prayer cylinders abound and the monks religiously turn them as they pass. These monasteries are always interesting places to visit.

But neither in them nor in the villages and towns of Ladákh does one meet with the Buddhism of romance.

Along with much that is quaint and weird and fascinating from an artistic standpoint, there appears to be only too much that is gross, sensual and depraved. Ignorance and pride as usual go hand in hand. There is no "Light of Asia" here. It appears to be passing scarce even in Buddhist countries.

28. ROCK PICTURE AND INSCRIPTION AT KHALATZE.
(Date 200-300 B.C.)

CHAPTER XI

THE UPPER INDUS VALLEY

Khalatze Fort and Bridge—An Ancient Inscription—Ruined Castles — The Moravian Mission — Tsongkapa, the Reformer — Ririzong Monastery—Potted Lámas—Alchi Monastery—Bazgoo—The Mongol War—Leh, a Town in the Desert—Dogra Conquest—Moravian Mission Work—Buddhist Chortens and Rock-Carving—The Hemis Demon Dance—Evangelization of Tibet.

LEAVING Lámoyóro we descend into a narrow valley, passing on the way some very remarkable lacustrine deposits on our right. These cover an area of several square miles and present very much the appearance of a large glacier, only, instead of ice or snow, there is a crevassed surface of hard and smooth clay. The height above sea-level is about 11,000 feet. Following a deep gorge, with precipitous sides, for about two hours, we emerge in the relatively broad Indus Valley, just below Khalatze, where there is an interesting old fort guarding a bridge across the river. Near this bridge there are many boulders of a deep red colour polished by the sun heat and drifting sand of ages. Some of these show traces of ancient carving. The ibex is a favourite figure. On one stone there is a more elaborate representation of a tiger chasing some smaller animal and an inscription in Indian Brahmi of the Maurya period. This stone was discovered by the Rev. A. H. Francke, a Moravian Missionary, who was working in Khalatze, and at his request I photographed it and a print was sent to Calcutta to Dr Vögel, by whom it was deciphered and found to indicate the fact that as long ago as 200-300 B.C. the Indus was crossed at this place (Plate 28). This is the most ancient stone inscription in Ladákh.

K

At Khalatze there is a ruined Dard castle, with in front of it a short inscription in Indian character. Some earlier inscriptions which have been found at Khalatze are thought by Mr Francke to belong to the times of the ancient Mons.

Western Tibet was colonized by Indians at a very early period, as is shown by the inscriptions in Brahmi characters dating as far back as 200 B.C. Tradition has it that at a great council held by King Asoka in the third century B.C., Buddhist missionaries were to be sent to Kashmir and even Yarkand. By the second century A.D. Buddhism was firmly established in Kashmir and had also probably penetrated Western Tibet. It is thought that the colonies of Mons, which are found in so many of the villages of Western Tibet, may be the descendants of those early Indian colonists.

The Dard dynasty seems to have ended about the end of the twelfth century. At that time the country was divided among many petty rulers who were continually at war. And especially at harvest-time perpetual raids and counter-raids were made. This accounts for the large number of ruined castles in which stores of grain were kept and to which on alarm the non-combatants fled, and if hard pressed the combatants also. And yet a through trade was carried on down the Indus Valley. Mr Francke recently explored and excavated the ruins of Balu Kar, an old customs-house on a precipitous knoll overlooking the river a short distance above Khalatze. There used to be a bridge at this point. The customs-house was fortified and its officer had the title Mdo gtsong gtso—Lord of the trade in the lower valley. Mr Francke found a number of ancient beads, and also some very old tea, but no coins.

Bragnag Castle, which crowns the rocky cliffs above Khalatze, was built by King Naglug about 1170 A.D. And a bridge over the Indus was constructed at the same time, evidently in opposition to that of Balu Kar, which is 3 miles further up the valley. The object was doubtless to make a rival customs-post and secure a share of revenue from the trade which passed through.

In the Indus Valley traces of gold-diggers are abundant. All along the banks between Khalatze and Saspool there are signs of old diggings and in some places there are the ruins of buildings. Mr Francke found that in Khalatze there were old folk tales about gold-digging ants, reminding one of the stories of Herodotus.

The Moravian Church has a Mission Station here, and for some years Christian work has been steadily carried on among the villagers. Mr Francke's name is a household word in Khalatze, and since he left, the Rev. S. Ribbach, one of the most capable and devoted of the Moravian Missionaries, has been working the district. The moral influence of the Mission is most important, although so far very few Ladákhis have actually become Christians.

From Khalatze the route lies up the Indus Valley, which is here 9500 feet above sea-level. The road, except where it is driven down to the river by cliffs, crosses a series of arid plateaus intersected by deep ravines. One of the commonest plants in the scanty herbage of these desert uplands is the wild caper, with its white hellebore-like flower, solid green buds and fleshy leaves. Nine miles beyond Khalatze there is a very narrow gorge on the left. Four miles up this, quite off the beaten track, is the interesting monastery of Rirdzong, belonging to the reformed Tsongkapa or yellow sect. Tsongkapa was born in 1355. He was the great reformer of Lámaism, which he found very corrupt. He tried hard to persuade the Lámas to again wear the yellow robes of Buddhism and he also sought to improve their morals, which were then, as now, very bad. After encountering much opposition and carrying on a vigorous controversial campaign, his cause became increasingly successful in Central Tibet and large numbers of followers adopted the yellow cap of early Buddhism, the badge of his party, which he called Gelugpa—the sect of virtue.

In Ladákh he was less successful. At present there are two sects of Lámas, the red and the yellow. But both wear red robes, and the only difference in dress is in the caps and girdles, which in the case of the red sect are red, and in the other yellow. The robes of the early Buddhists were yellow. Even now some of the Lámas in Zanskár, between Kashmiri Tibet and Kishtiwár, are clothed entirely in yellow.

In Central Tibet the yellow sect is now much larger than the red. And Tsongkapa's name is almost as sacred as Buddha's. His image, with characteristic tall yellow mitre, is conspicuous in all the temples of the yellow sect. Tashi Lunpo at Shigatze, the home of the Tashi Láma, was founded by Tsongkapa's nephew in 1445, and contains a large pillared hall with a huge statue of the reformer, who is regarded as an incarnation of Amitabha, and is supposed to have been reincarnate in the present Tashi Láma.

Rirdzong Monastery is a very large building. It is unusually clean and well kept and much more modern than most, being hardly a century old. This monastery has a better moral reputation than most.

Retracing our steps to the mouth of the gorge, a march of 14 miles through a very desolate part of the Indus Valley, brings us to Saspool. This is a large village with about 3 square miles of cultivated land, irrigated by a large stream, in which there are numbers of small snow trout. A few hundred yards above the village are the ruins of an extensive monastery, which was probably destroyed in the Balti War of the latter half of the sixteenth century.

On the walls of numerous caves which remain there are still frescoes in a wonderful condition of preservation, and we found several clay medallions stamped with the image of Buddha. These are said to have been prepared from the ashes of cremated Lámas or Buddhist priests, and they are prepared by adding a little clay and stamping them with a large seal. A chance traveller once called them

29. ALCHI TEMPLE.

With image of Buddha and wall frescoes, showing Lotsava, the founder.)

"potted Lámas," a suggestive, if somewhat irreverent, name.

Opposite Saspool, on the opposite side of the river, there is a village called Alchi, about 3 miles away, which contains the oldest monastery in Ladákh, one of the original Kashmiri Buddhist Lámaserais.

This monastery at Alchi is noteworthy because it is one of four which were built by Kashmiri monks, the most famous of whom was Lotsava Rinchen bzangpo, who is said to have lived in the year 954 A.D. In one of the rooms of the temple there, I was able to obtain a good photograph of an ancient wall painting, representing this monk (Plate 29). The characteristic feature of these ancient Kashmiri monasteries is the employment of richly carved wood. At Alchi, in front of the temple, there is a verandah with substantial wooden pillars surmounted by beautifully carved capitals on which there is a cornice similarly ornamented. Above this are smaller pillars and arches with trefoil design and images of Buddha and Buddhist saints. The doors, too, have very broad frames which are carved in Kashmir style. On the walls, both inside and out, there are numerous paintings. Mr Francke says that there are monasteries presenting similar characters at Kanika in Zangskar and Sumsa, Manggyu, Chigtan and Bazgoo.

From Saspool the road leaves the Indus and climbs up a steep ravine to a plateau. After about 5 miles there is a steep descent to the village of Bazgoo, which clings round the foot of a rocky ridge which is crowned by the ruins of an extensive fort which was erected by Dragspa, brother of King Lde the Reformer. Bazgoo was sacked by Zoráwar in 1836 in the second Dogra war. The rocks here are of a rich red colour, and the whole place is exceedingly picturesque. In the foreground are some immense chortens, with máni walls, said to have been erected by Stag tsang ras cheng, a very famous Láma, who lived about the end of the sixteenth century, and is believed to have introduced the custom of building these walls into Ladákh. In the little valley there is a clear stream surrounded by fields of barley and groves of poplars and willows, and there is also an orchard of apple trees. Behind is the bold outline of a rocky ridge with the ruined castle and a Lámaserai. At the foot of the cliffs are a considerable number of flat-roofed houses with prayer flags fluttering in the breeze, and prayer wheels being turned by the stream. The mountains around are beautiful and are the home of ibex, wild sheep and snow leopards. On the plain just beyond Bazgoo, a great battle took place about the middle of the seventeenth century. The King of Western Tibet, who was at war with Chinese Tibet, asked help from the Moghuls, who were then reigning in Delhi and held Kashmir. Shah Jehan sent an army which crossed the Indus at Khalatze on two wooden bridges and advanced to Bazgoo. The Mongols had taken up their position on the Plain of Jargyal between Bazgoo and Nyemo. They were signally defeated and decamped, leaving the field of battle strewn with primitive weapons, armour and baggage.

In return for this aid the King of Ladákh had to promise to become a Mussulman, build a mosque at Leh and to give Kashmir the monopoly of the wool trade. Unfortunately as soon as the Moghuls had returned to Kashmir, the Mongols again descended and King Delegs had to buy *them* off next by agreeing to pay yearly tribute.

Leh, the capital of Ladákh, is situated 20 miles further up the Indus Valley. It is a town in the desert (Plate 31). The desert, however, is not a plain but a sloping valley surrounded by barren mountains, and with the green margin of cultivation stretching only just so far into the arid wastes around, as irrigation can be carried from the stream upon which the life of Leh depends. Twelve miles behind Leh, the valley is closed in by a snowy range, which is crossed by the Khardong Pass, 17,400 feet above sea-level and 6000 feet higher than Leh. This is the route to the Sháyok, Nubra valley and Yarkand. Below Leh, the valley

Photo by] [*R. E. Shorter.*

30. VIEW FROM THE PALACE, LEH.

opens out into a fan-shaped expanse of desert extending down four and a half miles to the Indus River. Owing to the extraordinary clearness of the atmosphere the distance looks much less. Close to the river there is an isolated rocky hill the upper part of which is terraced with the white buildings of the monastery of Spittag. This, which was built by King Lde under the influence of Tsongkapa, was the first of the reformed monasteries. Later on others of the same sect were founded by subsequent kings. One of these, Trigtse Monastery, 12 miles further up the Indus Valley, is placed in a very commanding situation on the top of a rocky peak.

The view from Leh across the Indus is magnificent (Plate 30). In the distance, but looking quite near, is a line of snows culminating in a peak over 20,000 feet in height. The prevailing colour of the numerous ridges below snow level is light red. In the early morning and at sunset the play of colours is sublime: the mountains glow with shades of orange and crimson, while their shadows are often a pure liquid violet. Spittag, with its picturesque monastery, the walls of which catch up the sunlight, the village nestling in verdure, and the broad stretch of desert in the foreground and middle distance flanked by rocky heights, combine to form a picture never to be forgotten. The atmosphere of the valley is remarkably clear and transparent, and the heat of the sun very great. There is generally a difference of more than 60° between the reading of the exposed sun thermometer *in vacuo*, and the air temperature in the shade, and this difference has occasionally exceeded 90°. Dr Cayley succeeded in making water boil by simply exposing it to the sun in a small bottle blackened on the outside, and shielded from the air by inserting it in a larger phial of transparent glass. Owing to the diminished pressure of the atmosphere at the elevation of Leh, this would, however, take place at 191° or 192°, or about 20° below the normal boiling-point at the sea-level. The average rainfall is only three inches a year. Leh itself is a remarkable town, and is the meeting-place of Aryan and Mongol, the western centre of Lámaism and an important mart for Central Asian trade in wool, tea and Indian hemp. Here may be met traders from many remote districts, and the streets are full of picturesque figures. Leh is a town of flat-topped, terraced houses built of sun-dried bricks. There is one broad street with a line of poplars and quaint two-storied houses, in the shops of which all sorts of bright-coloured garments and other goods are exposed for sale. This street is also used for polo, and exciting games are played by enthusiastic Tibetans mounted on the small active country ponies. The main street is entered at the south end by a large gateway. At the other end is the steep slope of a rocky ridge with terraced houses and a very large chorten with a white dome and red spire. Crowning the whole and high above the town is the most conspicuous building of Leh—the palace. This is nine stories high. It is said to have taken three years to build, and was constructed by King Senggenamgal early in the seventeenth century (Plate 31).

On top of the hill behind the palace there is a red monastery containing a colossal image of Matreiya, 25 feet high, the head of which projects above the floor of the second story. This was erected by King Lde.

Leh was invaded by the Dogras under Zoráwar in 1835. The following winter the Ladákhis revolted and attempted to throw off the Dogra yoke. This led to another invasion by Zoráwar, and the King of Ladákh, whose name was Tsepal, was deposed and sent to live at Stog, a village on the other side of the Indus. Zoráwar built the present fort, and put in a garrison of 300 men. He then left the country after sacking the king's treasure house.

Once more in the winter of 1840-41 the Ladákhis rose in rebellion. This was quickly subdued by Zoráwar. In the following year, however, this redoubtable general lost his life in a campaign against Central Tibet. For the

31. LEH, A TOWN IN THE DESERT

Tibetans found a valuable ally in the intense cold. The armies met on a plateau 15,000 feet above sea-level not far from Gartok. The Dogras had already suffered severely from the snow. The fight lasted for three days. The Tibetans then made a charge and a horseman speared Zoráwar, who had already received a bullet wound in the right shoulder. Thus perished a gallant soldier, who had served his master, Goláb Singh, well, and made his name to be feared throughout the whole of Western Tibet.

Goláb Singh did not accept this reverse as final. A fresh and well-equipped army was sent up to Leh, and from there it marched to Drangtse, near the western end of the Pangong Lake, and after damming up the stream so as to flood the Tibetans out of their entrenchments the Dogras delivered their attack and completely routed the Tibetans, capturing their leader, whom they promptly executed. Having thus vindicated their authority, the Dogras then made peace, taking Ladákh as the spoils of war and once more finally allotting to the king the village of Stog and its petty revenue.

In Leh there is now a British political officer, who is on the staff of the Kashmir Residency. The administration is carried on by a Governor appointed by the Maharajah of Kashmir, who is grandson of Goláb Singh.

Since 1875 the Moravians have had a Mission Station here. They have had a succession of earnest and capable missionaries. The Rev. F. Redslob, the founder, was much liked by the people, and exerted a great influence for good. The Mission Hospital attracts large numbers of sick people, and is much appreciated. Typhus fever often breaks out in epidemic form in Leh and the villages around, and causes terrible mortality. Both Mr Redslob and Dr Marx, the Mission doctor, lost their lives from this disease in 1891; and in 1907 Dr Ernest Shawe, who had succeeded Dr Marx and had been attending large numbers of typhus patients, also died of typhus. The whole history of the Moravian Mission in Ladákh is one of noble self-sacrifice and devotion, for the climate is most unsuited for the prolonged residence of Europeans owing to the extreme altitude. Nevertheless, the work has been steadily carried on by Mr Weber, then by Mr Ribbach, and at the present time by Messrs Peter, Schmidt and Reichel. There is now a small community of Tibetan Christians.

About a mile above Leh there is an immense chorten, the largest in Ladákh. This was erected by King Lde. Close to this the Moravian Missionaries, who were carrying on excavations, found a large grave with many ancient skeletons and painted clay-pots apparently dating from the time of the Dards. This chorten was perhaps built to antagonize the spirits of the old Dards, which were supposed to bring death and disaster.

A few miles beyond Leh, in the Indus Valley, is the large village of Sheh. Immediately outside Leh, on the road to Sheh, there is a very long mani wall nearly half a mile in length with high chortens at each end. This was constructed by King Deldan in the first half of the seventeenth century. A very large chorten at Sheh, five stories high, was also erected by the same king. On the rocks at Sheh, just where the path from Leh reaches the Indus, there is a remarkable image of Matreiya, about 30 feet high, which is thought to have been sculptured by order of King Nyima Gon about 975 A.D. There is also an inscription showing that at that time the Buddhist religion was fairly established in Western Tibet. It was not until the fourteenth century that Lhassa became the religious centre for Western Tibet also. From that time the Bon religion disappeared, but the Buddhism of Tibet became less Indian.

Buddhism was first introduced into Central Tibet about 400 A.D. Rather more than two centuries later, this religion began to spread rapidly owing largely to the influence of King Shrong Tsan Sgampo, who was a zealous proselyte,

But for another two centuries there was an acute struggle between it and the Bon Chos.

The chief emigration of Buddhism from the Kashmir side is believed to have taken place between A.D. 600 and 1000, and to have been then due to a general decay of Buddhism in the valley of Kashmir which resulted in the impoverishment of the monks and impelled them to move eastward.

Rather an absurd episode occurred as I was entering Sheh. I was riding a local pony. These little beasts sometimes strongly object to umbrellas. And I was carrying one, as the sun was intensely hot. For some miles all went on well. But when nearing my destination, I turned round to see whether the baggage ponies were in sight. In doing so my umbrella must have moved forward a little. The pony at once bolted and charged straight into the coolie who was carrying my tiffin basket. And we all fell in a heap together. No one was hurt, but the injured expression on the coolie's face was most amusing.

The monastery of Hémis, which is situated about 20 miles further up the Indus Valley, is nearly 12,000 feet above the sea-level. It is especially famous on account of the great religious masquerade which is held there every summer. There are about 300 Lámas in the monastery, which is really quite a settlement. Hundreds of spectators are drawn from Leh and scattered villages far and near. Many of the women appear in richly-coloured silk dresses, and on the appointed days it is a strange sight to see the crowds of pilgrims making their way up the desolate and barren desert slopes to the scene of the dance.

THE LÁMA DEVIL DANCE AT HÉMIS

The object of this dance is probably chiefly to illustrate the struggle of the demons for the soul of man, and the value of priestly intercession. It is performed in a large courtyard surrounded on three sides by verandahs (Plate 32). On the fourth side a colossal banner, with a representation of the founder of the monastery, was hung. This is only exhibited once in twelve years. The following is an account of the day's dance at which I was present. It will be seen that it was somewhat monotonous, although quite unique, and remarkably interesting. Every available space, whether window, verandah or housetop, was crowded with Tibetan spectators. About 9 a.m., after a few preliminary growlings from the shawms (copper trumpets 15 feet in length), suddenly the band struck up—cymbals, shawms, clarionets and drums forming the orchestra. The players were red-robed monks with dragoon-shaped red cloth helmets, and they faced a broad flight of steps on the opposite side of the quadrangle. Down these steps two figures (acariyas) made their appearance, clothed in yellow-brocaded costumes with masks of cheerful aspect and red handkerchiefs over the back of their heads. In their hands each had a stick with a tuft of hair on the end. With these they kept the crowd in order, and also carried on by-play—behaving like circus clowns.

Next thirteen richly-dressed figures with black hats (rather like large stiff Tam o' Shanters) came dancing down the steps. On top of each hat there was an erection about 10 inches in height with a tiny model of a skull in the centre. Each dancer had a handkerchief tied over his mouth, a piece of skull in his hand, and a life-size picture of a skull suspended in front of his rich robes. These black-hatted devil dancers proceeded to hop round in a circle—revolving from right to left and left to right alternately on each leg to an accompaniment of quiet singing and measured beating of drums and subdued clash of cymbals by the band. Two Lámas now came forward and gave a little brush of twigs to each dancer, and then placed a small image on the ground and a pan of live charcoal. A Láma remained standing by this, holding a bunch of peacocks' feathers in his hand. The black-hatted ones now danced round slowly, waving coloured silk rags

Photo by] [*R. E. Shorter.*

32. THE LÁMA DEVIL DANCE AT HÉMIS.

round their brushes. Quiet singing by the Lámas was continued. Then clarionets sounded from the top of the steps, and the dancers slowly went off in that direction.

After this there was a pause of five minutes, during which a steady, low, measured beating of drums and cymbals was carried on. Then the clarionets sounded out and sixteen figures trooped on, clothed in rich costumes of Chinese brocade—some blue, others red, green and yellow. They had flat brazen masks, tall caps, and each held in his left hand a small bell and brass sceptre (dorje), and in the right a tiny double drum (daru). The leader's drum was white, all the rest were green. The band sings, the dancers step to right and left, close in, form a smaller circle, rattle their drums and bells, and after measured chanting they caper round. Two trumpets are now blown on the steps and they run off two by two. More quiet singing is carried on by the band. It is now half-past ten. Then there is a pause, only broken by low drumming and occasional reinforcement by cymbals and clarionet. The abbot of the monastery now rings his bell, and while the band plays loudly he sprinkles his desk and seat with holy water. Another Láma sprinkles the ground in front of the shrine. Then all the musicians respectfully stand at attention as a procession of sixteen unmasked mitred Lámas enter. Each of these carries a little bell, a sceptre and a tiny double drum. And each has his mouth tied up with a handkerchief. They are attended by acolytes in yellow aprons. Following them come several figures with very large yellow, red, black and green masks and rich robes—the Founder of the Monastery with attendant spirits good and evil. Over the Founder a large umbrella-like canopy is carried. These sit in a row against the east side of the quadrangle. The Lámas sing and continuous drumming goes on.

Suddenly high piercing, weird whistling was heard and a troop of demons with flags on their heads trooped in, scampered round and ran off again. The Lámas continued their singing. The two acariyas again began to carry on by-play. Then four young drummers, unmasked, with crown-like head-dresses, came in, and facing the Founder and his attendant spirits proceeded to make a curious humming noise while one beat his drum and the others pretended to do the same. This went on for a long time and then the drummers marched off. Next a blue-faced spirit began to dance, holding a sceptre in the right hand and a bell in the left. A benevolent white-faced spirit now came out and danced. Then the Founder, with a little drum in his right hand and a brass box in the left, and dressed in a white silk-flowered gown, did the same. After this a red-faced spirit danced, holding a little drum in the right and a large spoon in the left hand. Next an orange-faced demon, with a spear and flag and metal spoon in his hand, executed a dance. The band continued playing. Then a blue-haired devil dancer with yellow robes pranced about. Next a blue-faced tusked demon came out and danced. He was shortly joined by two equally hideous attendants who danced in step with him. Then a black-haired, black-faced figure took his turn and was joined by two equally horrible attendants. After this the sixteen mitred Lámas who had been sitting in the centre of the court paid their homage to the Founder and sang softly without accompaniment. The clarionets now sounded on the steps and the whole of the dancers and mitred Lámas marched off to the sound of drums, shawms, clarionets and cymbals. After a great noise from these, sudden silence supervened.

It was now about 12.30, and there was an interval of an hour, during which some Lámas and some also of the spectators prostrated themselves before the colossal picture of the Founder. Occasionally, too, the shawms were blown.

At 1.30 a black-faced demon entered with a representation of a skull, life-size, hanging in front of him, and holding a red-and-black flag in his right hand. Then a row of ten hideous demons, horned or black-hatted, with little skulls on the crown, came into the arena. These wore long capes of many colours. One held a naked sword, a second the model of a human heart, another a sickle, a fourth a hammer. Others held spears, chains and models of human viscera. These were to represent the devils who struggle for the human soul. Two ape-like figures with gaping mouths now rushed on and joined in. The Lámas continued to chant and the drums to beat. Finally the demon figures went off, two by two, to the sound of shawms and cymbals. After a short burst of music, an offering in a brass vessel was made to the shrine by a Láma, who prostrated himself. A mat was now deposited in the courtyard with a tiger skin in the centre. A procession of the abbot and attendant Lámas approached this. The abbot, clothed in a yellow cloak, held a silver cup; one Láma by his side carried a ewer and another a plate. Standing on the mat, amidst soft singing and chanting, the abbot rings a little bell in his left hand and, his head being bare, thrice fills the cup from the ewer and pours the fluid out on to the ground. He then puts on his hat and places a banner on the floor. Then a weird and shrill whistling arises and four death's-head maskers, clothed in white, rush in and dance near the banner. One of these holds a small skull in his hand and a stick with a blue flag. A violet cloth containing a model of a human figure is now placed on the banner on the ground by a Láma. The death's-head maskers go round and round this their victim, make signs over it, and then run off two on each side. Drumming and beating of cymbals goes on, and then a yellow-faced and hideous demon enters, a second with a red face, a third green, and a fourth white. One has a sickle, another a chain, a third a rope. These dance round and round and go off to the sound of the clarionets. Drumming goes on. Then a procession of Lámas enters—two with censers, one with a ewer, two with clarionets, and a horrid red devil with white hair. The red devil has a sword which he waves as he approaches nearer and nearer. The Lámas move off, leaving him alone. But he is now joined by four more—three red-faced and one black—with pictures of skulls hanging in front of their robes. These dance round the victim. The musicians of the band chant—the demons walk round in procession. Drums and cymbals beat. Then there is a pause and they begin again. A Láma now cuts up the image and gives a portion to each demon. Lámas chant again and the demons strike a listening attitude. Two clarionets sound on the steps and the demons troop off two by two. It is now 3.10 p.m.

After a pause of about ten minutes a red demon enters, followed by others, red, yellow, green and white, each with a death's-head on his breast and four of them crowned with skulls. These dance round and Lámas sing. They continue dancing, and finally a Láma distributes portions of the image to them and then carries off the mat, figure and banner.

A yellow demon with a white flag on his head beats a drum on the top of the steps. He is joined by figures dressed up as yellow tigers and with flags and small skulls on their heads and bells round their waists. These ran about wildly, went off and came on again. They then formed themselves into two rows of five each, facing each other. While one of them beat a drum the others pretended to do so—beating time with their drum sticks but not touching the drums. They advanced and retreated and crossed over from side to side. This went on monotonously for a long time. After about half an hour the whole ten struck their drums loudly and with a steady rhythm of one long and three short strokes for about twenty minutes. The Lámas chanted and suddenly the demons howled and ran round the arena. Trumpets were blown and then a silence supervened. It was now 4 p.m. and all was finished.

Tibet is one of the countries the door of which is still closed to evangelistic effort. It was hoped that the result of the recent expedition would have been to open it not only to trade but to Christianity. So far those hopes have not

Photo by] [G. Millais.

33 INTERIOR OF CHAPEL IN BUDDHIST MONASTERY.

been fulfilled, and the British Government is very averse to any travellers entering the country.

It is greatly to be regretted that in spite of the expenditure of life and treasure, Chinese Tibet is more closed than it was before the war. This is characteristic of the unfortunate methods of British policy. The recent invasion of Tibet by China will seriously alter the political equilibrium of Central Asia and cannot fail to affect India. It seems probable that what has been refused by Britain may be granted by China, and that in future the best route to Chinese Tibet and Lhassa will be through China, and that missionary effort may be directed from that side with greater hopes of success than in time past.

Meanwhile there is plenty of work to be done in Western Tibet and on the borders. And there are points of contact, and influence is being brought to bear upon the people. For many years the Moravians have been carrying on a quiet work among Tibetan-speaking people to the south and west. And there are several centres with small Tibetan Christian congregations. Not long ago a Láma, touched by the kindness shown to him by the missionaries when he was ill, and impressed by a study of the Gospels which had been given to him, became a Christian. He has, I hear, exercised great influence on his former disciples in Western Tibet, and it is possible that several may ere long join the Christian congregation.

Mr Francke, who formerly worked in Khalatze in the upper Indus Valley, brought out a monthly newspaper in Tibetan. The circulation was small so far as the number of copies issued was concerned; but each copy was handed on from one to another, and the monasteries furnished not a few regular readers.

On the east side on the Chinese border a quiet work is going on at Ta-Chien-lu and other places. A most interesting book, *With the Tibetans in Tent and Temple*, by Dr Susie Rijnhart, gives a graphic description of work in Tankar and Kumbum monastery, and a record of an heroic but disastrous attempt to penetrate to Lhassa, the great centre of the Láma system, in which she lost both husband and child, the former being murdered by robbers. Although the journey was rash, we cannot but admire the zeal and self-sacrifice of these pioneers. Who can say that such lives were really lost in vain? Tibet will become open to the Christian Faith in the course of time. At present, opposition emanates mainly from the Láma priests. The monasteries are great land-holders; and so the weight of wealth, the influence of priestcraft, and the traditions of a religion which has existed many centuries, combine to form a citadel which will require very much more extensive effort than is now being put forth, before it shows signs of capitulation.

The Kashmir Mission of the C.M.S. occupies one of the outposts of the Church of England on the Indian Frontier. Further east are the Moravian Stations. This is the fighting line of Christianity and it is a very thin one. The battle is prolonged. There can be no doubt as to the result if the Church is only true to its trust. The results of Mission work are indeed according to our faith, not only as individuals, but also as a Church. The lack of men and means, of which we hear so much, are symptoms of want of faith, and yet how much there is to be done. India is still feebly occupied by the Church, and Central Asia is practically untouched. Where are the men?

CHAPTER XII

SPHERE OF INFLUENCE OF MEDICAL MISSION WORK

Racial Antagonism—Points of Contact—Opportunities for Service—Economic Value of Medical Relief—Should Missionary Work be Supported?—Aims and Attainments.

Such mercy He by His most holy reede
Unto us taught, and to approve it trew
Ensampled it by His most righteous deede
Shewing us mercy, miserable crew!
That we the like should to the wretches shew
And love our brethren.

SPENSER.

THE rapid development of India has brought us face to face with many grave problems. The action of the National Congress, the Swadeshi movement, the Pan-Islamic revival, and the anti-British tone of a large section of the Indian Press, are various manifestations of this. It has, however, been truly pointed out by the Bishop of Lahore that the very rise of these new conditions is, in large part, due to our National Christianity and to our attitude toward and manner of dealing with India. As missionaries, our one aim is to bring India the very best (of all which we believe that we have received from God) of faith and high moral and intellectual ideals and of self-sacrificing service. That mercenary motives are often imputed to the British, whether Government servants or missionaries, is too true. On the whole we believe that imputation to be both unjust and untrue. Missionary enterprise has done more to keep steadfastly to the front the highest principles and motives of life, than any other agency in India, and it has achieved results too extensive to be measured. It is not too much to say that

Indian Society, whether Hindu or Mohammedan, is unconsciously saturated with Christianity. Many missionaries who are lamenting their apparent want of success and who deplore the comparative rarity of the crowning joy of individual work, the actual receiving of convinced and consistent Christians into the visible Church, would be much happier in their work if they could only realize the extent to which they have been permitted to be the instruments of disseminating the highest truth.

We believe the present state of India to be a stage of progress, and that the best and truest of our rulers have indeed been striving, as has been well said, "to do what was right from day to day, believing that if this were the principle of our rule, the ultimate issues of it could not be evil, or in any real sense injurious to ourselves."

If the time has come—or when it does come—that Indians should be permitted and encouraged to take over administrative and judicial responsibility, to a much larger extent than hitherto, I believe that missionaries will welcome such a change —a change which is not only inevitable but to be hoped for soon, and which might be at once safely realized, if only "the valiant man and free, the larger heart and kindlier hand" had been rung into the land to a larger extent than is the case.

Missionaries in North India are apt to feel that as Christians they have more in common with Mohammedans than with Hindus. The Mohammedan belief in the Unity and Purity of God and their theoretical acceptance of "the Law," seem to give a common platform of belief. It is important that the most should be made of these points of contact. We owe a debt to those who, like the eminent linguist, Dr Grierson, have emphasized the importance of the Hindu doctrine of Bhakti, the oneness of the Supreme Being, and the sinfulness and unworthiness of man, a doctrine, too, which recognizes Incarnation. "In every nation he has faith who feareth God and worketh righteousness, for he is accepted with Him. And the man that walketh in darkness and hath no light, if only he walks uprightly and judges righteous judgment, he, too, shall see the mystery of the truth and duty that he loved, unfolded in the loving face of Him, that liveth and was dead and is alive for evermore."[1]

One of the strong points of Medical Missions is this, that they enjoy exceptional facilities for showing kindness and courtesy to thousands of Indians of all classes, and of rendering service to them. One of the greatest duties and privileges of the British in India, is to set forth the honourableness of service and the nobility of "the golden rule"; ideas which, although deeply rooted in the West, have not yet received much acceptance in Asia, in practical life.

At the present time, when there is an undoubted increase of racial antipathy between East and West, it is most important that all Englishmen should set themselves determinedly to extend more kindliness and sympathy to their Indian neighbours and dependents, and to do what they can to lessen the bitterness and racial dislike, which are becoming so painfully apparent.

Another strong point of Medical Missions is that they aim high. The highest ideal of life is for us to address ourselves to the task of carrying out the programme of Christianity, to cheer the poor with good tidings, to release the captives, give sight to the blind, and set at liberty those who are bruised. We have been privileged to see a partial realization of this ideal in our own age and our own country. How many hospitals, infirmaries and asylums have been founded for the relief of every kind of disease! In every city, too, how numerous are the benevolent institutions and the associations for improving the condition of the poor, the suffering and the degraded! It was not always so. What has made the difference? The growth of refinement and civilization? Surely not! There was a high degree of refinement and civilization in Rome and Athens in olden days, but little humanity. More than half the population of those

[1] Gwatkins.

cities was enslaved. And apart from military institutions, not only were there few if any hospitals for the care of the poor and suffering, but we know that, on the contrary, heartless selfishness and merciless cruelty flourished in the midst of civilization and refinement as in a congenial soil. Was the condition of things any better in India before the days of British rule? Was there any care for the sick poor? Were there any hospitals or institutions for the relief of those afflicted with blindness or other disease?

It is to Christianity that we must look for the great motive power of philanthropy. Its great Founder proclaimed His Mission to be for the relief of the distressed. It was He Who sent out His disciples with the great commission to heal the sick and say unto them, " The Kingdom of God is come nigh to you." He was never more at home than in a crowd composed of persons suffering from every kind of disease and infirmity of body and mind, " amongst whom He moved benignly, touching one here into health, speaking to another the word of power, and letting glances of kindness and good cheer fall on all." And, following in His holy footsteps, Christians have at all times carried on the great work of comfort and healing. Public hospitals, refuges for the blind, and asylums for lepers, owe their origin chiefly to Christians. In more recent times Christian statesmen brought about the abolition of slavery, and a Christian lady started the great Dufferin scheme for the relief of suffering women in India.

As the influence of Christianity has spread and become stronger, it has gradually altered the whole character of public opinion until, instead of, as in the classical days of paganism, its weight being on the side of cruelty and neglect, the scale is now weighed down on the side of mercy. And in these days Christian charity is not content with ministering to human misery, but seeks to remove its causes and to so regulate the conditions and environment of life as to avert the onset of disease. This great Christian influence spreads and radiates until we find, especially in the large cities of India, non-Christians, Parsis, Hindus and Mohammedans, whose consciences have been stirred and who are awakening to the needs of the distressed and suffering, and coming forward and liberally supporting or even founding hospitals and other institutions for the relief of disease and pain. But, although full of promise for the future, such instances are still exceptional, and as a whole, the Indian people are very far behind. They have little desire to engage in practical philanthropy and they care for none outside their own family or caste. And if charitable institutions are organized for them, those who are not Christians often cannot be trusted to administer the funds honestly. Nowhere does the gulf between East and West come out more clearly than here. On the one side we have apathy, callous neglect, and gross and often dishonest selfishness; on the other, the high ideals of Christian philanthropy. It makes one sick at heart to hear English men and women who openly advocate leaving the Hindus and Mohammedans where they are—English men and women who lightly esteem their own priceless heritage, the Christian Faith, handed down through centuries of struggle against wrong, and who so depreciate the moral and spiritual resources of the West as to think that we have no gifts to impart to the East. Have we no higher ideals of unselfish devotion to duty, of purity, of family life, brotherly love and charity to all men, than the seething mass of corruption, deceit, selfishness, impurity, fraud and intrigue with which the Indian peoples are infiltrated? We know we have. But the question is, how are these to be imparted? The only efficient way is for whole-hearted Christian lives to be lived in contact with the people. Precept is important. Christian educational work in India is most important. Preaching, too, is a divinely appointed method. Those are needed who follow in Christ's footsteps, upon whom is the spirit of the Lord as they go forth among the men and women of India to preach good tidings to the poor and proclaim the acceptable year of the Lord. But, above all, example is necessary. Those who are in Government service are precluded from, in their official capacity, promoting the spread of Christianity. But if they are Christians at all, they cannot help bearing witness by their lives and actions, and by their personal influence in private life. Contact with the people must tell.

It is here that the great value of Medical Mission work is manifest. It is following the highest example. Medical Missions are quite one of the most important manifestations at the present time in the whole world of the practical spirit of Christianity. They use medical science for its highest purpose. Taken at the lowest estimate they confer an enormous boon on suffering humanity, not only in India but in China, Africa, Persia, Arabia and other countries which are in great need of humanizing agencies.

So far as men and funds have been available, various Missionary Societies have endeavoured to carry on this important work.

The Church Missionary Society, for instance, through its Medical Mission Auxiliary, has planted out forty hospitals with a staff of eighty-six doctors and fifty-two nurses. In this way medical relief is being afforded annually to more than a million sufferers, to whom also Christ is set forth as the Saviour.

We often hear the objection that this work should be done in our own land where it is alleged it is more needed. It is done there. There can be no conflict between different parts of the Christian's work. Those who are most earnest and keen and devoted in work amongst the needy at home, are just the people who are most in sympathy with those working abroad. A living Church at home makes an active Church abroad. From a medical standpoint it appears that the need abroad is greater than at home. In Great Britain it is said that there is one qualified medical man to every 1400 of the population. In India there is not one to every

100,000. A distinguished officer of the Indian Medical Service has stated that it is doubtful whether five per cent. of the Indian population are reached by skilled medical aid. In London the mortality is barely twenty per thousand per annum. In Indian cities, even when there is no plague, it is quite double. In Kashmir about half the children born are said to die in infancy. As if the pain and suffering of the Eastern peoples were not sufficient, it is in many cases aggravated by neglect and apathy, or by the cruel and barbarous treatment of untrained native practitioners and ignorant impostors.

In Kashmir we are in the midst of a population of this kind, with its high mortality and all its suffering. Let us look at the work of the Mission Hospital from the standpoint of the people of the country. They know that in it they have a place to which they can go in time of need; that it is open to all, without distinction of race, creed or caste; that their religious feelings will be respected, and that when admitted to the hospital they will be treated with kindness, clothed, fed and receive personal attention, and the necessary surgical or medical treatment. They know that the institution is clean, well-ordered, and that they will have a large measure of freedom in receiving relatives and other visitors from their homes. Those who come from the valley also know that they will receive Christian instruction there. So far from considering this a reason for not coming, a great many of them welcome the teaching, and not infrequently express their appreciation of the friendly personal interest thus taken in them. In the wards of the hospital, with these hundreds of patients constantly in touch with Christian work and Christian teaching, we have that very contact of race with race, of Christianity with Mohammedanism and Hinduism, which is needed, and which is so beneficial, and which is essential if the people are to realize the nature of the Christian Faith and its claims upon them.

Last year there were 23,642 new out-patients and 1979

in-patients in the hospital. What becomes of all these people? They return to their homes. Many go to crowded streets and alleys of the city. Very many disperse to scores of villages scattered throughout the length and breadth of the valley of Kashmir, others to the plains of India, some few to distant mountain homes in Tibet, Afghanistan, and even Yarkand and Khotan. Herdsmen, peasants, shopkeepers, traders, landowners, priests, State officials—every class is represented, and so the work of softening prejudice, overcoming bigotry, and smoothing down racial distrust goes on; and in many a distant village, grateful appreciation is still retained for very real benefits received, for the saving of life, the restoration of sight, or relief from disabling pain and disease. And thus, too, attention has been directed toward the Great Physician, of Whose teaching such are the fruits. And step by step, slowly it is true, but surely, the way is being prepared for that Kingdom for the coming of which so many pray in one of the commonest but most sacred petitions.

"What a difference between such work and Bazaar preaching. In the bazaar, shouting and argument; the preacher contradicted, and Christianity and Englishmen alike reviled and held up to contempt. It is indeed a work which needs doing, but what gifts of tact and meekness are needed for it. In the hospital, on the other hand, quiet, gratitude, bigotry melting away, hard hearts thawing, Christ revered, Christian 'altruism' acknowledged and praised."[1]

The value, too, of medical work from the standpoint of political economy is of interest. Every disabled subject is a source of loss to the State. Agricultural or other work is left undone, or imperfectly done. Every patient, previously incapacitated for work, who is healed and restored to his occupation, is a distinct gain to the country. So that medical and surgical work directed in one year to the successful relief

[1] Dr A. Neve, *Mission Hospital Reports.*

of several thousand patients is of direct political importance.

There are not a few who do not, we regret to know, believe in what they call " the Missionary part of our work," but for the sake of the great amount of relief to suffering achieved by the Mission they give their cordial support. We do not expect those who are not Christians to approve of Christian Mission work. Such work is, however, carried on for the benefit of all classes, without any distinction of race or creed, and we are thankful for the help accorded by those of any class, whatever their religious beliefs may be. Philanthropic work forms a happy bond of union between those whose views on most subjects may be very widely divergent. Upon those, however, who are Christians, it is surely evident—unless their faith is purely nominal—that Medical Mission work has a very special claim—a claim not based on isolated texts from the Scriptures, but on the whole life, example and precept of the Master.

Whatever our opinions may be about Missionaries and Missionary methods there can be no doubt whatever in our minds, if we are Christians at all, that the duty of evangelizing the world is laid upon the Church.

So that such objections as that the evangelization of India or of Kashmir is impossible, or that it is undesirable, are simply irrelevant. For the question for us is not whether it is possible or desirable, but " What is the duty incumbent on Christians ? "

One of the commonest objections to Mission work in India is that the people's own religions are good enough, and perhaps better for them than Christianity. Such an objection can hardly come from Christian lips; for the declaration of, and witness to, the truth of our Faith is of the essence of Christianity. Moreover, an acquaintance with the religious beliefs of the country shows how defective they are in ethics, and how overladen with gross superstitions.

Those who are imperfectly acquainted with practical

Mission work often assume that the preaching and teaching of Christianity is disliked by the peoples of India, and is, so to speak, forced upon unwilling hearers by ignorant and more or less fanatical missionaries. This view would be amusing if it were not so generally current. It is certainly not the case in Kashmir. No doubt there are many amongst our hearers who are apathetic and listless. There are others who make no attempt to listen, who are too ill, in too much pain, poor things! too ignorant, or too certain that their own is the one true faith. And, of course, there are always some who are too worldly and sensual to even understand the teaching of Christ. But these raise no objection to the preaching, their attitude is rather one of indifference. On the other hand, there are many who are quite the reverse, who listen with attention, almost with eagerness, and some of whom audibly assent. It is by no means uncommon for patients in the wards to ask us to come and talk to them.

No, it is not the teaching they object to. It is the idea of changing their religion, of breaking their caste, and being formally, by the act of baptism, cut off from all their old associations and family ties. *There lies the crux.*

The fight with Mohammedanism is a stern one. The work goes on day after day and year after year, not only in Kashmir but in other Mohammedan countries, with very little outward sign of progress. The mass of the population appears to have so little desire for righteousness that it does not realize the inadequacy of Islam. Humanly speaking, Mohammedanism owes its origin in a measure to the unfaithfulness of the Christian Church of those days. It is a very serious question whether it does not owe its continuance in these days in almost equal measure to the same cause.

Nowhere is the need for Christianity greater than in Mohammedan lands. Nowhere is the challenge more emphatic for us to abundantly prove that the Christian faith alone has power to bear fruit.

The halo of romance which surrounds a sphere of work is

not always dispelled by closer contact. But when actively engaged in grappling with obstacles, the eye is focussed on near objects, and for a time more distant things are hazy or unseen. Thus it is with the routine duties and wearing details of Medical Mission work. Now it is the monotonous and brain-fatiguing claims of language-study that distract. Anon it is the exhausting demands of surgical practice under difficulties. Again it is the spiritual, moral and intellectual barrenness of the people, or the blatant and self-conceited ignorance of their teachers. Nor are there wanting foes from within. In a great undertaking, difficulties are inevitable. But the very obstacles in the path of progress spur the traveller to even greater effort. And when success has been achieved, then every drop of previous pain and toil is transformed into the very essence of sweetness, enhancing joy a thousand-fold.

CHAPTER XIII

DEVELOPMENT OF KASHMIR

Material Improvements—Influence of Medical Mission—Future of Kashmir—Probable Victory of Christian Faith and Ethics.

> Ring in the valiant man and free,
> The larger heart, the kindlier hand;
> Ring out the darkness of the land,
> Ring in the Christ that is to be.
>
> TENNYSON.

EVEN the quietest and most secluded spot cannot resist the tide of progress and advance which beats upon its shores. Kashmir is undergoing rapid changes. The prices of food have increased immensely. This may be borne with a measure of equanimity, when we recognize that our loss is the gain of the actual working-classes of the population. The liberal rates of pay offered by Government Departments have made both skilled and untrained labour more expensive and difficult to obtain. Difficulties of transport, too, in the valley may increase if changes in time-honoured arrangements are hurried on precipitately.

Visitors returning to the country, after an absence of a few years, find many material improvements—new houses, metalled roads, substantial masonry bridges, solid embankments and electric lights. Such changes at once strike the eye. But they are only an index to still greater reforms. The creation of the State Council, the inauguration of the land settlement and the reorganization of the Financial, Public Works, Postal, Telegraph and Forest Departments, have contributed largely to the material, and not a little, we may hope, to the moral welfare of the subjects of His Highness the Maharajah. And looked at simply from this standpoint, the growth and development of the Mission Hospital is worthy of some notice. This forms now one of the most important public buildings in Kashmir. Year by year it has increased in size to enable it to cope with the demands made upon its accommodation and resources by an ever-growing multitude of patients. During the past ten years 436,364 visits from out-patients have been recorded, 14,727 have been taken into the wards of the hospital as in-patients and half a million meals have been supplied free. The large number of surgical operations, 40,710, shows how far the confidence of the people has been secured. There is no doubt that the Kashmiris believe more in surgery than in medicine; the reason, of course, being that the results of the former are so much more tangible. The removal of a large tumour or the extraction of a "cataract" can be appreciated by the most ignorant, and the use of chloroform and other anæsthetics does much to remove the dread of the more serious operations. Surgically the success cannot be gainsaid. Year by year increasing numbers of sick are relieved, and a higher standard of work aimed at. Year by year, too, we see evidences, not indeed so tangible as surgical statistics, but as incontrovertible, that prejudices and bigotry are breaking down. We see racial and religious barriers yielding, and a new spirit at work.

Although the outlook for Kashmir is, on the whole, bright, there are some shadows. There is ample room for increase in the population. For immense areas may still be brought under cultivation. Famine will never again, under wise administration, assume the appalling proportions of the years 1878-9. Sanitation has had great victories in the past —notably the introduction of a supply of pure water to the city, whereby thousands of lives have been saved in subsequent cholera epidemics. In the future it will push these successes further, and also deal with the causes underlying the deficient female population. Much, for instance, may be effected by more careful and thorough vaccination.

Already there are signs of real danger from the rapid increase of tuberculosis in the valley. This will need to be vigorously combated, although the time is not yet ripe for the adoption of segregation measures. Leprosy also will have to be exterminated.

The low-lying ground round the Jhelum River will, it is to be feared, continue to be liable to serious periodic inundation. The catchment area is so enormous and discharges its waters so rapidly into the main stream, that the deepening of the river-bed at and above Baramula, although mitigating, will not prevent the occurrence of floods. It is a pity that the wisdom of King Asoka or the Emperor Akbar, in placing their respective capitals above flood level, was not imitated by the founders of, and more recent builders in, the present city of Srinagar, such important parts of which lie below flood level. Much can, however, still be achieved in the direction of draining and reclaiming swamps. Crops may be improved in quality, and a greater variety be introduced. With its copious water-supply, unlimited electrical power will be available in Kashmir when required for commercial use. The railway when constructed will give a great impetus to trade. Sooner or later the country will be thrown open to capital.

The northern races and those living in mountainous countries have in time past been those who have taken a leading part in history. Kashmir may have a great future before it. In physique and intellectual development its people compare most favourably with those of any part of India.

The administration is steadily improving; and as officers of better training and with higher ideals replace those of the old school, there will be still greater progress, and many tyrannical abuses which still exist will disappear.

The extension of education will also bring about great changes. At present the villages and outlying valleys are virgin soil. Female education, by bringing the earliest possible influence and training to bear upon the children, through their mothers, will elevate the race in health, mind and morals. Technical education has a great future before it. The Kashmiris are naturally clever with their hands. Careful instruction will improve the quality of the art work already produced. And fresh outlets will be found for skill.

Under favourable conditions, and especially if there were facilities for transport, such as a railway or even the projected cableway, much raw material might be prepared or manufactured for export. Various existing industries might be developed and fresh ones started, such, for instance, as basket-weaving, oil-presses, mills for cloth and linen, match factories, potteries, paper-works, tanneries, dye and soap works, saw-mills, rope factories and workshops for high-class carpentry and cabinetmaking.

Above all, the greatest advance is to be looked for in the direction of moral improvement. No amount of material prosperity or of ordinary education will, for instance, remedy the incredible amount of perjury which exists in Kashmir at the present time, and which comes to a focus in the law courts. A healthy public opinion is necessary. At present this is conspicuous by its absence. But Kashmir has been downtrodden for centuries and is only now emerging from mediæval conditions.

In this connection the subject of religion cannot be ignored. Kashmir is essentially a Mohammedan country. But Islam is not a regenerating force. The condition of Mohammedan lands is well known. And they all have a family likeness. For the defects of the system are more easily assimilated than its elements of loftiness. Modern Islam in India is at present engaged in putting new patches on an old garment. But the old garment will not last.

Indeed Mohammedanism in India shows curious traces of its prolonged contact with Hinduism. And at the present time it is being profoundly influenced by its Christian surroundings.

The new Mohammedan University, if conducted on modern lines, will accentuate this influence and tend to emphasize the nobler and Theistic aspect of the religion, the

Arabian founder of which will occupy a less important position as his limitations become more clearly recognized.

Hinduism has still great vitality and a remarkable capacity for the absorption of other religious systems and doctrines. Its time-honoured foundations, however, must eventually be sapped by the progress of education. It is only a question of time.

Kashmir will derive its moral springs of action more and more from Christian Faith and Christian Ethics.

This is not the mere dream of an enthusiast! The Car of Progress is moving slowly forward. It must not be made to travel too fast. In the East, reaction follows very closely upon precipitate action.

During the past quarter of a century the material, intellectual and moral advancement of Kashmir has, however, been great and altogether unprecedented in its previous history. And if even the present rate is maintained, the future of Kashmir will become increasingly hopeful and happy as the seed which is now being widely sown comes to fruition.